ESSENTIALS OF
AMERICAN BUSINESS

ROBERT J. WECHMAN, Ph.D.
Department of Business and Economics
BMCC, City University of New York
St. Thomas Aquinas College

ISBN 0-87563-342-0

Published By
STIPES PUBLISHING COMPANY
10 - 12 Chester Street
Champaign, Illinois 61820

TO

Stephanie

Craig

Evan

Darren

TABLE OF CONTENTS

PART FOUR - FINANCE

PART FIVE - OTHER ASPECTS OF BUSINESS

PART ONE

FOUNDATIONS OF AMERICAN BUSINESS

I
THE DEVELOPMENT OF BUSINESS IN
WESTERN CIVILIZATION

Since the beginning of mankind business was probably a main feature in his being. If he desired something another person had he would make an exchange with that person. Of course, that person would trade with him only if he had something that the other person wanted. This was called <u>barter</u>.

I. Ancient Egypt (e.g. 4000 B.C. - 1000 B.C.):
    a) In ancient times business was important to many elements of the society.
    b) The development of agriculture in ancient Egypt:
        1. The Nile River controlled the economic life of the country.
        2. Egypt was basically an agrarian country for the vast majority of the populace was employed in agriculture.
        3. Flax and cotton made possible the manufacture of linen and cotton goods.
        4. The Egyptians grew crops such as beans, peas, lettuce, cucumbers, barley and wheat.
        5. They had numerous vineyards, olive trees and date palms.
        6. Oxen and donkeys were their domesticated animals.
        7. The Egyptians main farming implement was the plough which was drawn by oxen and used by the peasants.
    c) The development of industry in ancient Egypt
        1. Since the Egyptians were able to grow more crops than they used themselves, they were in a position to exchange the surplus for copper mined in northern Arabia and on the island of Cyprus.
        2. The Egyptians imported wood from Syria, spices and incense from India, and iron from Asia Minor.
        3. Stone and brick were used for building purposes.
        4. Wooden boats were constructed when found desirable in order to extend trade from local areas to the coast of the northern Mediterranean Sea and the Indian Ocean.

5. The Egyptians exchanged raw materials for leatherwork.
6. They dyed linen cloth, manufactured glassware and pottery, made figures in copper and bronze and constructed beautiful furniture.
7. The building of the pyramids (which were tombs for the Pharoahs) was a type of welfare state. The subjects of the kingdom needed work so they shouldn't starve. Therefore, the government provided a government sponsored project.

II. Ancient Mesopotamis (e.g. 3000 B.C.):
   a) The Sumericans were very skillful in agriculture, taking full advantage of the fertile soil and the plentiful water supply.
     1. Sumerians raised grain vegetables and dates.
     2. Kept domestic animals such as goats, sheep and cows.
     3. Had a good dairy industry.
     4. Land was worked by tenants who rented the land.
     5. They had free laborers who worked for wages.
     6. They also had a system of slaves.
     7. Bread was baked.
     8. Linen was made from flax since flax and wool were produced in great quantities.
     9. Great height of business was before 3000 B.C.
    10. Men and women signed receipts, accounts, bills, notes and letters.
    11. Money was lent from 20 to 33 1/3% interest.
    12. Salesmen traveled from one city to another, for hundreds of miles.

III. Phoenicia (1200 to 350 B.C.):
   a) Located where Lebanon is today. Their land was too mountainous to make agriculture flourish. Because of this, the Phoenicians looked to the sea and trade to earn a living.
   b) The Phoenicians were fishermen and sailors and after 1000 B.C. they became the leading traders of the Mediterranean area.

3

c) The forests of Lebanon supplied them with timber and resin necessary for shipbuilding.
d) Many commodities from other lands were imported by the Phoenicians to be used as raw materials in their manufacturing.
e) Fine carpet, glassware, silver, bronze and desirable purple fabrics which were manufactured in the factories of Sidon and Tyre were exported to all parts of the known world.
f) The commerce of the Phoenicians had a large amount of piracy and the taking and sale of slaves was a profitable business for them.
g) The chief colony of the Phoenicians was the city of Carthage located in present day North Africa. In the 6th century B.C. Carthage was the largest city of the area with a population estimated at being in the neighborhood of 3/4 of a million people. This large population provided the Phoenicians with a large market for their goods.
h) The Phoenicians kept complete and concise business records.

VIV. Greece (e.g. 3500 B.C. - 300 B.C.):
a) Greeks saw trade as important in such Greek city states as Thens, Sparta, and Syracuse.
b) Though the Greeks saw trade as important they looked down on businessmen. If you were of pure Athenian blood you did not become a merchant.
c) In Plato's Republic the businessman was not given a high position in Plato's idea of the perfect state. He was given a very low position in Plato's state.
d) Because they were looked down upon in many of the city-states, merchant cities such as Corinth which was located on the Greek peninsula, gave merchants respect and protection.

V. Rome (e.g. 500 B.C. - 476 A.D.):
a) Empire organized under Roman governors who helped to implement a codified international law which helped to improve trade.
b) Banking and speculation developed under Roman rule.

c) The Roman economy was based on slavery, which ruined many of the small farmers causing unemployment and leading to a drift of population to the cities.

d) Julius Caesar (49-44 B.C.) introduced many administrative reforms to improve the collection of taxes, cut the grain dole by 50%, redivided land, abolished imprisonment for debt and cut taxes. By abolishing imprisonment for debt and cutting taxes, Julius Caesar encouraged people to try their hand in various businesses.

e) In the Roman Empire many business people flourished. They were given government contracts to build fortifications, public buildings, aqueducts and collect taxes. Many merchants also made tools, armaments, jewelry and pottery.

f) There were a number of economic reasons for Rome's decline:
   1. Over-taxation of middle class resulting in its ruin.
   2. Rise of slavery.
   3. Exhaustion of the soil.
   4. Extravagance of court.
   5. Decrease in population.
   6. Trade fell off - unfavorable balance of trade.
   7. Growing gap between the rich and the poor.
   8. Peasants lost farms and flocked to Rome where they lived in slums.
   9. Inflation.
   10. Scarcity of precious metals for currency and exchange.

VI. Medieval Europe:

With the fall of the Roman Empire in the Fifth Century A.D., Europe fell into turmoil. By the tenth century A.D. the governments of Europe disintegrated and central government and common protection of the citizens ceased to exist. Great landholders became a law unto themselves. Because the governments were unable to rule all the territory nominally subject to it, they gave immunity to many monasteries or lords. When the king gave immunity, he renounced his right to collect taxes and maintain law and order. The continued incurions of the Norseman, Saracens and Magyars left each local area to fend for itself.

Because of these events, Feudalism developed.
Basically feudalism was a system of protection in return
for goods and services. It was also an economic system
of self-sufficients agricultural manors and land holding
in return for goods and services.

    a)   From the 11th century on there began to
be a growth of towns throughout
Western Europe for a variety of reasons:

        1.   Some old Roman towns were
still in existence.

        2.   Crusades led to an increase in
business; this stimulated
the growth of many of the
old towns (especially in
Italy).

        3.   New towns sprang up near
monasteries, castles or at
the junctions of rivers.

        4.   Protection.

        5.   Trade.

        6.   Business.

        7.   Sudden increase in population.

    b)   Business of the town was controlled by
guilds:

        1.   Merchant Guilds (organization
of Trades) regulated
trade, imports, exports,
prevented competition, did
religious and charitable
work, organized the poli-
cing of the city and armies
for defense and set stan-
dards of conduct for their
members.

        2.   The guild was monopolistic –
only members of the guild
could practice the trade.

        3.   The purpose of the guild was
for the protection of the
interests of trade.

        4.   The guild controlled the
hours of work and the
quality and price of the
products.

5. Almost every kind of occupation belonged to the guild. In some French cities, even the prostitutes belonged to a guild.

VII. The "Just Price" in the Middle Ages:
   a) Many of the church writers, in the early middle ages, expressed doubts about the virtue of those engaged in commerce and wondered if they could achieve salvation. However, by the 12th century many of those associated with the Catholic Church saw that those who engaged in trade were providing an important service for the public.
   b) Therefore, the churchmen gave a moral justification for those who engaged in commerce. Businessmen who provided their goods and services without fraud and only sought enough of a profit to support themselves and their families were worthy of honor. Those who cheated and were too greedy were to be dishonored.
   c) By the 13th century the doctrine of the just price was developed. A price was looked upon as being just if it was close to being what the going price was, that is, the current market value. Later, as guilds regulated prices, another criteria for the just price was added. Prices had to conform to legally fixed rates. Prices were considered unjust only where one obtained a special advantage which was much higher than what the market price or the legally determined price would bring.
   d) Usury, the lending of money and the charging of interest was considered to be sinful by the Catholic Church. In theory this made banking an occupation which was impossible for good Christians to hold. In the early years of the Middle Ages, money lending was confined to Jews. Many people believed that the Jews were going to "Hell" anyway so they could engage in the business of money lending, since it didn't make a difference.
   e) During the Middle Ages, Jews were not allowed to own land and engage in the practice of agriculture. Therefore, many Jews went

into the business of moneylending. Jews
were subject to the mercy of the local lord.
They had no rights except what he was willing to give them. Many lords looked upon
Jews as a profitable investment. Whenever
the lord wanted or needed money, he simply
taxed the Jews whatever he desired. In
England, whenever a Jew died, 1/3 of his
property went to the king. This was common but the king was able to take whatever
he wanted, whenever he wanted, by any
method he desired from the Jews living in
his realm.

f) The Hanseatic League was formed in the 13th
century by the cities of northern Europe for
the purpose of maintaining trading agents in
major cities for the protection of trade from
thieves. The Hanseatic League, with membership of over seventy cities, controlled
many trade routes throughout Europe. The
Hanseatic League played a major part in the
commercial development of Western Europe.
It fell into decline with the development of
New trade routes.

g) Medieval Fairs were international markets for the
exchange of goods. The fairs had a system
of coinage, bills of exchange, laws of commerce and standards of weights and measures.

IX. The Commercial Revolution:
a) Events that brought about the Commercial Revolution:
1. Crusades.
2. Marco Polo.
3. Capture of Constantinople in 1453.
The capture of Constantinople
in 1453 by the Ottoman Turks
helped change the course of
history because this event
closed Europe's access to Asia
and the East and therefore another route had to be found.
Because of this event Columbus
went on his voyage to search
for an all water route to the
east in order to obtain an increase in trade.

b) Effect of the Commercial Revolution on Europe:
   1. Increased trade.
   2. New Products (potato).
   3. Overseas market (New World).
   4. More powerful middle class.
   5. Domestic system of production.
   6. Increase in use of money.
   7. Decline of Feudalism.
   8. Slavery reintroduced into Europe.
   9. <u>Rise of Mercantilism</u> - government has complete control of the economy of the country. The wealth of a nation is measured in the amount of gold and silver it possesses.
   10. <u>Growth of capitalism</u> - a system of private enterprise based on risk and competition.
c) The Commercial Revolution influenced the course of American History:

Crusades
↓
Growth of Towns
↓
Trade { Manufacturing (Manufacturers and traders needed products to be sold abroad)
↓
Finance
↓
Business Organization }
↓
Ottoman Turks capture Constantinople
↓
Search for an all water route to the East
↓
America

X. Finance and the Growth of Capitalism:
   During this period of time there was a significant amount of changes in commerce, agriculture and industry in Europe. Because of these changes a financial system had to be developed to handle them.
   Throughout the 16th and 17th centuries there was a shortage of precious metals and many European governments prevented them from being exported. Minting methods were primitive and there was a great deal of counterfeiting and debasement of coinage occurring at

that time. This hampered business. Queen Elizabeth made some attempts to stabilize the English currency but this only achieved limited success.

An increase of bullion during this period of time led to a growth in the amount of coinage being minted. Silver was the most used of the coinage. Toward the end of the 15th century, silver coins were heavily minted to replace other kinds of coinage. Gold did not become heavily minted until the 18th century. Many European countries started using copper in the minting of coins. There was a great deal of cheap metals being used throughout Europe in the small retail trade with the growing use of commercial paper for larger businesses.

From the late medieval period in Europe there grew the custom of balancing books and paying creditors by using letters of exchange. Many merchants at the great markets (called "fairs") of Europe established a theoretical standard of value which was represented by the use of paper money. This paper money was used in many areas of Europe in place of the different kinds of coinage. The success of this type of paper money is believed to have helped lead to the development of banks in Amsterdam, Hamburg and Nuremberg. The merchants took the coins that they received to these banks and exchanged them for credit which was given in the form of bank money or paper money. This bank money became very popular among merchants because this type of money was relatively stable.

Goldsmiths were the chief bankers of England before the establishment of the Bank of England in 1694. The goldsmiths kept money and valuables in their vaults and collected rents for their customers and took money for deposit. The goldsmiths paid interest on the money they kept on deposit. The goldsmiths gave "goldsmith's notes" which circulated as "bank money" in England because the English had faith that the goldsmiths would pay money upon demand. To reduce the amount of counterfeiting the goldsmith's introduced a checking system which grew so rapidly that by the 18th century the goldsmiths who were known also as bankers had to establish a clearing house for the checks.

The payment of debts by the exchange of paper grew quickly. This led to the commissioning of third parties (usually a banker) to collect the money. This led to the French bankers establishing the system of endorsement (the signing on the back of the letter of exchange). By the endorsement the right of one person to a particular amount of money was able to be transferred to another.

10

The development of public banking, the large acquisitions of capital and the chance for large profits led to a lowering of the interest which was paid on commercial loans. From the middle of the 16th to the middle of the 17th century the average interest on most commercial loans was between four and six percent.

The steady amount of growth in coinage (a great amount of bullion came to Europe from America) stimulated commercial and financial activity but produced hardships on those who received wages and lived on interest or rent. This led to an inflation which caused the laboring classes of Europe to suffer because their wages were often fixed by government statute and therefore could not keep up with the inflation. This problem influenced many of the laboring class to migrate to the new world during the 17th century.

The growth of commerce, agriculture, industry and financial institutions with the increase in the amount of precious metals led to increased speculation and the growth in the amount of capital accumulated. Many merchants left their businesses and engaged in the area of financial speculation. Many merchants made as much as sixteen percent in monetary exchange operations.

The increase in the accumulation of capital was accompanied by a growth in the spirit of capitalism. This was a change from the medieval concept of the community to the concept of the individual. The capitalistic spirit stressed rationality, carefully planned business enterprises, the development of double-entry bookkeeping and the growth of a new code of business ethics. "To the new bourgeoisie, time was money, and character counted for much in the development of a successful business. Young men were urged to be frugal, industrious, and respectable, to strive for virtues which, incidentally, aided in the accumulation of capital and assured them good credit ratings." (see Tschan, Francis J., Grimm, Harold J. and Squires, J. Duane, Western Civilization Since 1500, New York: J. B. Lippincott Company, 1947, pgs. 551-601. This is an excellent discussion on the economic and social changes of the early modern era.)

QUESTIONS FOR REVIEW AND DISCUSSION

1. Describe the development of industry in ancient Egypt.

2. Why did the Greeks look down at businessmen?

3. How did Julius Caesar encourage Roman businessmen to flourish?

4. Explain feudalism as an economic system in Medieval Europe?

5. How was the business of the medieval towns controlled by the guilds?

6. Explain:
   a) Just Price
   b) Usury
   c) Hanseatic League
   d) Medieval Fairs

7. How did the Commercial Revolution influence Europe?

8. Why did paper money come into being in Europe during the 16th and 17th centuries?

9. How did goldsmiths help develop the English banking system?

10. How did the increase in coinage lead to the migration of the laboring class to the new world during the 17th century?

11. Explain what is meant by "the spirit of capitalism?"

II
BRIEF OVERVIEW OF THE DEVELOPMENT OF THE
UNITED STATES ECONOMIC SYSTEM

I. The Colonial Era:
 a) Colonies were overwhelmingly agricultural in nature.
  1. Items such as wheat, cotton and tobacco were the leading crops.
  2. There were small industries. Work was done by sole proprietorships who were artisans who produced a piece of work from start to finish.
  3. Most trade was done among the various colonies. This was done mainly by barter (the exchange of goods and services without the use of money) because settlers came from different lands (such as England, France, Spain, Sweden, etc.) and there wasn't a standardized system of coinage.
 b) The British colonies were run on the mercantile system.
  Mercantilism means that a colony exists for the benefit of the mother country and a nation's wealth is measured by the amount of gold and silver it possesses and there is strict government control of business.
 c) The U. S. Constitution (1787) was developed in great part to solve many of the economic problems that the new nation faced upon the conclusion of the Revolutionary War in 1783. The Constitution helps business by fixing a system of weights and measures, regulating coinage, regulating trade and tariffs, bankruptcies, etc.

II. The Industrial Revolution (e.g. 1790-1860)
 The Industrial Revolution came to the United States from Britain. In the 1790's Samual Slater brought plans of machinery to this country. With the advent of the Industrial Revolution in the United States one sees that machines replaced

13

individual labor with the workplace moving from the home to the factory. Also developed in this period was the division of labor which led to increased production. Eli Whitney, the developer of the cotton gin also was very instrumental in developing the idea of the standardization of parts which played a major part in the development of American industry.

Industry grew during this period because of demand for new products, sufficient labor due to newcomers continually coming to the United States from Europe, growth of overseas and domestic markets, government encouragement to industrial development such as protective tariffs and the building of canals and turnpikes, lack of regulation and many ambitious entrepreneurs. This period was emphasized by the growth of mass production with the simultaneous development of the specialization of labor.

III.   The Industrial Age (1865-1917)
      This period was highlighted by the settlement of the West, the building of the transcontinental railroad and the enormous growth of American industry featuring entrepreneurs and the growth of big businesses featuring monopolies and corporations replacing individual proprietorships. During this period, industrialists such as Harriman, Stanford, Carnegie and Rockefeller dominated the American scene. This period was also known as the production era because of emphasis being placed on developing and improving the methods of manufacturing.
      Due to heavy immigration to this country, there was a growing demand for manufactured goods that surpassed many manufacturers' ability to produce the goods. The continuous flow of immigrants provided an ever-growing domestic market for products and with the development of clipper ships, steamships and government support overseas, trade expanded. By World War I the United States was one of the most powerful industrial and trading nations in the world. During this period there was also attempts by the federal government to stop monopolies, regulate trade, regulate money supply and have business behave in a responsible manner. Because of this desire, Congress passed such acts as The Interstate Commerce Act (1888), The Sherman Anti-Trust Act (1890), The Pure Food and Drug Act (1906), The Clayton Anti-Trust Act (1913) and the Federal Reserve Act of 1913.

IV. The Twenties, Depression and World War II:
        After World War I the United States was elevated
to one of the most powerful nations in the world. In
the 1920's there was great growth of United States'
trade and industry. The Harding, Coolidge and Hoover
administration's took a laissez-faire (government stay
out) attitude toward business and business prospered
along with the rest of the nation.
        However, in 1929, along with the rest of the
industrialized nations, the United States went into a
depression. This depression lasted through the 1930's
until the U. S. entry into World War II. Because of the
depression, the Franklin D. Roosevelt Administration
adopted a policy of stricter government regulation over
the stock market industry, the banking industry and
giving labor more power. Such acts as the Securities
Exchange Commission Act and the Glass-Steagall Act
which created the Federal Deposit Insurance Corporation
and the National Labor Relations Act were passed.
        During this period, many in government adopted
the philosophy of John Maynard Keynes which believed
that the national government should regulate and intervene in order to fine tune the economy. Keynes believed that government intervention would help bring
about full employment. However, during peacetime there
has never been full employment by any President's
administration using Keynesian philosophy.
        During the period of the 1930's American business-
es concentrated on selling and advertising and the strong
pushing of their products upon the consumer.

V. The Post World War II Age (1945 - present)
        President Harry S. Truman maintained the Frank-
lin D. Roosevelt concept of greater government regulation of business. President Eisenhower reverted back
to less government intervention and President John F.
Kennedy and President Lyndon Johnson were in reality
Keynesian Presidents believing in governmental intervention into the economy. In addition, this period saw
a growth of marketing research in order to satisfy the
needs of the customer. After World War II American
business adopted what has been called the marketing
concept. This was a philosophy that stated that business should identify the desires of the consumer and
satisfy these desires in order to earn a profit.
        Beginning about 1960 the United States began
changing from being primarily a manufacturing nation to
becoming a service and information society.

With the advent of the Reagan Administration there was a large movement toward a policy of deregulation that had as its object the lessening of governmental regulation of business so that competition would be increased and American business could compete more successfully on an international level with foreign manufacturers and therefore reduce an unfavorable balance of trade.

QUESTIONS FOR REVIEW AND DISCUSSION

1. Explain mercantilism. Discuss its advantages and disadvantages.

2. Is the United States Constitution an economic document? Why?

3. How was the production era different from the marketing era?

4. During the industrial age, how did the United States government attempt to regulate American industry?

5. How much regulation should the government have over United States business?

III

THE ECONOMIC BACKGROUND OF AMERICAN BUSINESS

I. Economics
    a) Economics is derived from the Greek language and means "the management of a household."
    b) It is the study of how man uses his resources to produce goods and services in order to satisfy the scarcity of man's resources.
    c) Economics is the study of how goods and services are distributed within the society.
    d) It is the study of man's wants and the satisfaction of these wants.
    e) It is the study of allocating limited resources with unlimited wants.
    f) Economics is the study of the various activities dealing with how man earns a living.
    g) Economics is the study of allocating scarce resources.

II. It is an accepted fact that every person has particular wants and desires that he wishes to satisfy. In order to satisfy these wants, he must work. A business firm is usually the source that produces the want-satisfying good or service. Whether for good or evil, man's business activities have an affect on society.

III. Economic Law
    a) A law in economics is similar to a law in physical or biological science, in that it is a relationship between cause and effect. However, in the field of economics, one is dealing with human beings, not inanimate objects. Human beings do not always act in accordance with economic law.
        e.g. Under most conditions, a reduction in the price of a particular good will result in an increase in its sales. However, a retailer may find that a reduction in the price of a commodity will result in a decrease in its sales. This could occur if the retailer's customers believe that a low price means that the goods are inferior.

If this is the case, the retailer would probably be better off if he maintains higher prices. Therefore, an economic law is a statement showing that there is a tendency for an economic result to take place if certain economic events occur;

i.e., if this happens, then the following result "should" or "may" follow.

b) One of the basic tenets of economics is that the resources of anyone (whether powerful or not) is limited, and because of this, everyone has difficult choices to make.

1. The supply of oil is finite (limited). Therefore, a scarcity of oil would force mankind to make some tough choices. Should we keep our homes warmer in the winter and live closer to the job because we don't have oil for the automobile? If we produce the same amount of automobiles, should we cut the production of refrigerators?

c) A popular explanation of economics is "the study of how best to use limited means in the pursuit of unlimited ends."

IV. Adam Smith (1723-1790)

a) Wrote his classic work Wealth of Nations in 1776.
b) This work has become the backbone of free-enterprise ideology.
c) Adam Smith believed that:

1. All restrictions on industrial and commercial enterprise should be removed and the market should be allowed to work freely.
2. "Laissez-faire" - let things be - government stay out of business affairs.
3. All men have the natural right to own and protect their property.
4. All men are by nature materialists.
5. Man is a rational being and therefore would attempt to achieve a degree of material satisfaction.

a.   Competition and mutual self-interest will keep prices down as much as possible and encourage production to rise.

b.   Competition and mutual self-interest will serve to encourage man to make as good a product as possible for as reasonable a price as possible so that can maintain his customers in the face of his competitors.

6.   Adam Smith spoke of the "invisible hand" which means that business by doing good for itself, does good for the consumer.

7.   Adam Smith also took the position that people acting in their own self-interest in the economic marketplace would benefit all of mankind.

V.   David Ricardo (1772-1823)

a)   Was an English economist who as a utilitarian.

b)   Wrote Principles of Political Economy.

c)   Wrote about the "Labor Theory of Value." "The value of a commodity, or the quantity of any other commodity for which it will exchange, depends on the relative quantity of labour which is necessary for its production, and not on the greater or less compensation which is paid for that labor."

d)   Ricardo believed that man will place his capital (money) where it is to his greatest advantage. This idea has been expanded into what is presently called comparative advantage and absolute advantage.

e)   Ricardo believed that in the state of nature, exchange value varies directly in relation with the amount of labor input. Every increase in the quantity of labor adds to the value of that particular commodity.

f)   Ricardo's "Iron Law of Wages" show the economic law of supply and demand. He believed that an increase in population will lead to lower wages because there will be more labor available. Because of this, misery will result, but this misery will cause a reduction in population and therefore there will be less labor available and wages will then again rise above the subsistence level. When this happens, population will then increase again and the cycle will be repeated again and again. Therefore, labor's wages fluctuate from just below the amount needed to buy their subsistence to just above the amount necessary to purchase enough for subsistence.

Ricardo believed that wages should not be raised arbitrarily because nothing would be accomplished since the number of workers available would be greater than the supply of food.

g) Ricardo believed that wages were subject to rise and fall for two basic reasons:
    1.   Supply and demand of laborers.
    2.   The price of the commodities on which labor's wages are spent.

h) Ricardo simply took the position that the only remedy to solve the wage problem was to curb the growth in population and therefore decrease the supply of labor.

VI.   Karl Marx 1818-1883)
    a) Marx was a German political and economic philosopher. After the revolution of 1848 in which Marx was an agitator, he was forced to leave Germany. He finally settled in Great Britain, where he lived the balance of his life. In London, he devoted himself to various activities dealing with international revolution and to writing critical analysis of the capitalistic economy.

Marx worked with Frederich Engles who was quite wealthy and therefore supported Marx when Marx had difficulty providing food and shelter for his family. Their chief writings were The Communist Manifesto and Das Kapital.

Marx began following the philosophy of Frederich Hegel when he was at the Universities of Berlin and Bonn. Hegel took the position that as the institutions of a society mature they create opposites or antithesis. Out of the clash between the two opposites

20

a new society or what Hegel called a synthesis is created. The new synthesis becomes
a new thesis and the whole process, called
the dialectic, is repeated again and again
until perfection is achieved. Hegel believed
that by this dialectic, society progresses.
Karl Marx accepted Hegel's theory of progress. However, Marx had one fundamental
difference with Hegel. Hegel believed that
God was the controlling force of society.
Marx did not accept God. Marx believed
that the mode of production conditioned the
general character of all aspects of life.
Marx believed that the material, not the
ideological was the chief historical determi-
nant.

b) Dialectical Materialism

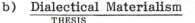

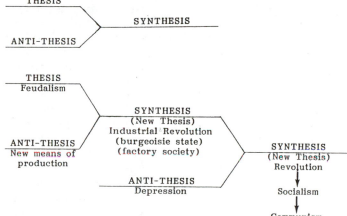

c) Karl Marx put the dialetical method of Hegel to
work in a materialistic context to create the
concept of dialectical materialism. Whereas
Hegel had looked upon human history as
emerging out of a process of conflicting
ideas, Marx and Engles looked upon history
as a conflict of material forces. This idea
has become known as historical materialiam.
Marx and Engles believed that the world of
ideas is built upon the material world. According to Marx, the state is the organization of the interests of the class that owns
the means of production. A class is any
group with the same economic interests.
Marx saw society as a war between the

proletariat (working class) vs. the bourgeoisie capitalist class). Marx believed that eventually the capitalist class would be defeated by having the means of production taken away from them.

d) Marx believed in the economic interpretation of history. He believed that economic conditions determine the course of history. He said that the class that possesses economic power controls the society. In a factory society, the capitalist class is the one who controls the society.

e) Marx also believed in the class struggle. In a free enterprise, society based on private ownership, the classes which are in the struggle are the bourgeoisie class vs. the proletariat class.

   1. Marx also believed that the workers in a capitalist society received a wage just a bit more than necessary to maintain their subsistence. Marx saw a difference in the value of the goods that the workers produced and the wages that they received from the capitalist. Marx said that the capitalist did not pay the workers enough. He called this excess that the capitalist took, surplus value. He said that even though the workers were responsible for the surplus value, it was taken from them by the capitalists for a profit.

   2. Marx believed that under capitalism, the rich would get richer and richer while the poor would get poorer and poorer. Marx believed that eventually the proletariat (working class) would revolt against the capitalists and establish a single class society under the rule of the proletariat with all the means of production placed under the control of the state which would be controlled by the ruling class, which would of course be the working

class. Private property would be abolished and the government would wither away.

f) Criticisms of Marx

1. Marx said, "From each according to his ability; to each according to his needs." He did not state who would determine what an individual's ability is and how much each individual needs.

2. Marx also stated that the conditions of the working class would get more miserable and miserable under the capitalist (free-enterprise) system. However, in reality the conditions of the working class has become better and better instead of becoming worse.

3. Marx also predicted that the middle class would become smaller and smaller under the capitalist system. However, he was wrong in this prediction. Under the capitalist system the middle class has become larger.

4. Since the entrepreneurs (the capitalist) are performing a major function in the system, such as taking risks, investing capital, organizing the factors of production and creating employment for the working class, Marx is wrong when he states that profits are stolen by the capitalists from the working class.

5. The establishing of a Marxist Communist dictatorship in the Soviety Union and its satellite countries has shown that communism severly deprives man of freedom rather than increasing his freedom. Under communism the workers have less to say say in regard to what they can or can't do than they have under a capitalistic (private enterprise) system. In the Soviet Union the workers are told what they can or cannot do, whereas in the United States the worker is free to choose the job he wants and to change jobs when he wishes.

23

6. Karl Marx also showed a lack of understanding of the human element. People wish to be rewarded for their efforts. People who show individual initiative wish to be compensated for it. Under communism they are not. Theoretically, under communism, everything is divided equally among the workers. However, in reality, this does not work. If people do not get rewarded for their efforts they will not work as hard or be as strongly motivated to perform. Marx did not understand this. In studying economic development, it is obvious that a free enterprise system such as that in the United States economically far outperforms a communist system as that in the Soviet Union.

VII. Joseph Schumpater (1883-1950)
   a) Schumpater was a German economist who immigrated to the United States and held a professorship at Harvard.
   b) His key works were Theory of Economic Development, Business Cycles, The Sociology of Imperialism and Capitalism, Socialism and Democrary.
   c) Schumpater was a romantic capitalist.
   d) Schumpater believed that capitalism was good because the competitive system absorbed the complete energy of most people at all economic levels. Because of this, much less energy is expressed in war and conquest than in any precapitalistic society. This is because the people's energy is used up trying to earn money.
   e) Schumpater believed that "the national economy ...is impoverished by the tremendous excess in consumption brough on by war." Therefore, Schumpater believed that it was not in the interest of the capitalist class to have war.
   f) He was in favor of free trade and pointed out that capitalists favored free trade.
   g) Schumpater strongly disagreed with Karl Marx; "it is not true that the capitalist system as such must collapse from immanent necessity,

24

that it necessarily makes its continued existence impossible by its own growth and development. Marx's line of reasoning on this
point shows serious defects, and when these
are corrected the proof vanishes."

h)   He also disagreed with the beliefs of Lenin:
"Export monopolism does not grow from the
inherent laws of capitalist development. The
character of capitalism leads to large-scale
production, but with few exceptions large-
scale production does not lead to the kind of
unlimited concentration that would leave but
one or only a few firms in each industry...
it is a basic fallacy to describe imperialism
as a necessary phase of capitalism, or even
to speak of the development of capitalism
into imperialism...Tariffs sprang from the
financial interests of the monarchy. They
were a method of exploiting the trader...
They were in line with royal perogatives of
safe conduct...of the granting of market
rights, and so forth. From the 13th century
onward this method was progressively re-
fined in the autocratic state, less and less
emphasis being placed on the direct monetary
yield of customs revenues and more and
more on their indirect effect in creating
productive taxable objects....The trading
and manufacturing bourgeoisie was all the
more aware of its dependence on the sover-
eign since it needed his protection....Inso-
far as commerce and manufacturing came
into being at all, therefore they arose under
the sign of monopilistic interest."

QUESTIONS FOR REVIEW AND DISCUSSION

1. Describe the different ways one can define economics?

2. What is an economic law?

3. Why is Adam Smith considered to be a great defender of free enterprise?

4. Explain Ricardo's "Iron Law of Wages."

5. Explain Marx's theory of the dialectic.

6. Why do many people say that Marx's philosophy is un-realistic?

7. Why was Joseph Schumpater called a romantic capitalist?

8. Who has been the most influential in the development of American business thought: Amda Smith, Karl Marx, David Ricardo or Joseph Schumpater? Why?

IV

THE FOUNDATIONS OF BUSINESS

I. In the United States business consists of all profit-
    seeking activities that provide various goods and
    services for the needs and desires of a society.
    a) Profit occurs when a company's income
        (receipts) are greater than its expenses
        (disbursements).
        1. Profit = Total Revenue minus
                     Total Cost
                 P = TR - TC
        2. Loss is when a business's ex-
            penses are greater than its
            revenue.
    b) Goods are tangible items that one can see,
        touch or hold - e.g. bread, radio, auto-
        mobile, etc.
    c) Services are useful activities that other peo-
        ple provide for us - e.g. physician,
        plumber, accountant, etc.
    d) Consumers are those who purchase goods
        and services.
    e) Producers are those who provide goods and
        services for the consumer.
    f) The marketplace is where the sellers and the
        buyers come together in order to ex-
        change goods and services for a con-
        sideration, usually money.
    g) Competition is the effort of two or more
        businesses to obtain the patronage of
        the same customers.
    h) Pure competition occurs when no business in
        a particular industry is dominant.
        Therefore, no single business in that
        industry can individually influence the
        price which is charged in that specific
        market.

II. The United States has a free (private) enterprise system.
    a) Private enterprise system is also known as the
        free market system and the free enterprise
        system. This is an economic system based
        on freedom of choice and freedom of competi-
        tion among business firms attempting to meet
        the wants and needs of society. It is also
        the belief in the principle of privately owned

businesses competing freely in the economy without government control.

b) <u>Planned economy</u> – is an economic system in which the government plans and regulates in economy. The government decides what should be produced; how the goods and services will be produced and for whom the goods and services will be produced.

c) <u>Mixed economy</u> - is an economy system which is a mix of private enterprise and government ownership.

d) <u>Demand-side economics</u> is the belief that putting government money into the economy will stimulate demand.

e) <u>Supply-side economics</u> is the belief that stimulating the various parts of the productive process such as savings, capital investment and productivity by lowering taxes will ultimately improve the nation's economy.

III. In all societies, economics must deal with three basic economic questions.
  1. What goods and services should be produced?
  2. How will these goods and services be produced?
  3. For whom shall these goods and services be produced?

a) The answering of these basic questions centers about the economic law of <u>supply and demand</u>.
  1. <u>Supply</u> is when the seller is willing to sell his goods on services at a certain price level at a certain time.
  2. <u>Demand</u> is when the buyer is willing to buy goods or services at a certain price at a certain time.
  3. <u>Law of supply and demand</u> is an economic principle or law that states that if supply is greater than demand the buyer has an advantage because there is a tendency for prices to go down. If supply is less than demand, than the seller has the advantage because there is a tendency for the price to rise.
  4. <u>Price</u> is the value which is put on a particular good or service.

5. Supply curve - shows the relationship between a particular price
   and the amount of goods and
   services supplied at that price.
6. Demand curve - shows the relationship between a particular price
   and the amount of goods and
   services demanded by the consumers at that price.
7. Equilibrium - is the point where the
   suppliers and demanders agree
   on a price. It is at that point
   that demand and supply are in
   balance.
8. Capital is money which is used to
   make the machinery or items
   which produces more money.
   Some examples are:
   a. the reaper for the
      farmer
   b. the machine that shapes
      shoes
   c. the loom that makes
      shirt material.
   Capital is also commonly referred
   to as the funding, usually
   money or credit that enables
   a business organization to
   operate a business.
9. Capital goods are man-made goods
   that are used to produce other
   goods. Some examples of these
   are machines such as those used
   to make automobiles and clothing
   and raw materials such as iron
   and fabric.
b) Under the American system, capitalism, which is
   a system of private ownership and control
   of the means of production, is viewed as the
   basis of the American economy.
   An honest capitalist is a benefit to society and
   should be respected as such. He or she
   should not be degraded, abused, tormented
   and hounded as if he or she did something
   evil in making a profit (a profit is the return on an entrepreneus's time, effort, investment and risk). An honest profit in an
   honest busines is a noble accomplishment
   and should be respected as such. Profit

29

produces capital, which leads to investment, which leads to productive jobs, which leads to benefits for all of society.

IV. Key terms dealing with business costs
    a) Explicit costs are costs in the form of money paid out - e.g. monetary payments made to a construction company to put an addition on to one of the company's buildings.
    b) Implicit costs are particular costs that are not shown as actual payments of money. For example, an entrepreneur puts in a great deal of overtime running his business but he does not receive money. In this case the entrepreneur is putting in his time and effort. This is an implicit cost.
    c) Short-run costs are those costs incurred in that period of time in which the productive capacity of a factory cannot be increased or decreased. For example, a factory can increase its production in the short-run by putting its workers on overtime and getting more material for the workers to use in the productive process.
    d) Long-run costs are costs in which the productive capacity of a factory can be increased. This can be done by adding a building to an existing factory or by installing new machinery. In addition, in the long run companies can enter the industry or leave the industry. It has been said that "all things are possible in the long-run."
    e) Variable costs are costs which can be changed in the short-run. For example, labor and energy are variable costs. They can be used to increase the amount of production that a factory can turn out in a short peri- of time.
    f) Fixed costs are costs which do not change if there is either an increase or a decrease in the amount of production that a factory puts out. For example, if the factory costs down its production, the company still has to pay interest costs or rent costs or mortgage costs.
    g) Total costs are fixed costs plus variable costs. FC + VC = TC.

h) <u>Marginal analysis</u> is used to determine if it pays
to increase production.

i) <u>Marginal cost</u> is the cost of producing one additional unit of an item.

j) <u>Break-even analysis</u> is used to determine the
level of activity at which an organization will
neither lose money nor make a profit. At
this level, the organization is operating at a
zero-profit level or break-even points.
Break-even analysis uses revenues, fixed
costs and variable costs.

$$\text{Break-even Point} = \frac{\text{Fixed Costs}}{(\text{Price} - \text{Variable Costs Per Unit})}$$

k) <u>Profit-volume analysis</u> uses the concept of marginal analysis. This is done because profit-
volume analysis defines costs and profits using fixed and variable costs. By keeping
the selling price and the variable costs at a
steady amount, entrepreneurs may be better
able to predict profits at various levels of
sales.

l) <u>Law of diminishing returns</u> states that if one
fixed factor of production (land for planting
of corn) gets added to it a variable factor
(man hours of labor), the yield from the
additional man hours of labor will be less
and less bushels of corn per acre of land.

m) <u>Economies of scale</u> means that the more units
you produce of an item, the less expensive
it is to produce each unit.

n) <u>Diseconomies of scale</u> means that the more units
you produce of an item, the more expensive
it is to produce each unit.

o) <u>Marginal Revenue</u> is the additional amount of
revenue (money) received by a firm by selling one additional unit of an item.

p) <u>Normal profit</u> is the lowest amount of profit an
entrepreneur receives in order for him to
remain in business. If the entrepreneur
does not make at least some profit, he will
not be able to remain in business.

q) <u>Rule of profit maximization</u> states that you will
be able to maximize its profits by producing
an item until you reach the stage where
marginal revenue is equal to marginal cost
(MR = MC). For example, one can continue
to produce an additional item if its costs
you $5.00 to produce the item and you re-
ceive at least $5.00 in revenue for the item.

31

However, if it costs you \$5.00 to produce the item and you only receive \$3.00 in revenue for the item, you will be losing money and therefore, you should cease producing additional items.

r) Gross National Product (GNP) is the measure in money of total goods and services in the economy.

$$GNP = C + I$$
$$GNP = \text{Consumption plus Investment}$$
$$GNP = C_{PE} + I_{GPD} + G + (X - M)$$

GNP = Personal Consumption Expenditures + Gross Private Domestic Investment + Government Expenditures + (Export - Imports)

s) Net National Product (NNP) is the gross national product minus depreciation on capital investments.

$$NNP = GNP - D$$

QUESTIONS FOR REVIEW AND DISCUSSION

1. How is competition different from pure competiton?

2. How is a private enterprise system different from a planned economy?

3. Which do you favor, demand-side economics or supply-side economics? Why?

4. Which of the three basic economic questions is the most important? Why?

5. Why is the law of supply and demand so important to the American economic system?

6. How is the supply curve different from the demand curve?

7. Why is capital so important to the American economic system?

8. Why is an honest capitalist a benefit to society?

9. How are explicit costs different from implicit costs?

10. Explain the difference between short-run costs and long-run costs.

11. How are variable costs different from fixed costs?

12. What is the purpose of break-even analysis?

13. How is economies of scale different from diseconomies of scale?

14. Why is the rule of profit maximization important in business planning?

15. How is gross national product different from net national product?

16. Why is marginal cost and marginal revenue so important in business planning?

17. How does marginal analysis affect business planning?

V

THE LAW AND BUSINESS

I. <u>Law</u> is a set of rules that determines the relationship of
    individuals and organizations to one another and to
    society. Law is the binding custom or practice of a
    society. It is the rules of conduct and/or action
    that a society wants enforced.
    a) Law is different from ethics because it is
        rules, statutes, codes, precepts and
        regulations which are enforceable by
        court action and enforced by the govern-
        ment.

II. Two main sources of law:
    a) <u>Common law</u> is a series of laws based on <u>stare</u>
        <u>decises</u> (precedents), which are past <u>deci-</u>
        sions of judges. Common law comes from
        England. It has become part of the United
        States legal system because it was brought
        here by the early English colonists.
    b) <u>Statutory laws</u> are all written laws passed by
        federal, state, county, city or other local
        legislative bodies - e.g. The U. S. Consti-
        tution, The New York State Constitution,
        gambling laws in Nevada, drinking laws in
        Connecticut and driving laws in New Jersey
        are examples of statutory laws.

III. Types of law:
    a) <u>Federal Constitution</u> sets forth the legislative,
        executive and judicial powers. Sets limits
        on federal powers.
    b) <u>Federal statutes</u> are laws passed by the United
        States Congress.
    c) <u>State constitutions</u> set forth the powers of state
        governments.
    d) <u>State statutes</u> are laws passed by the state
        legislatures.
    e) <u>Local statutes</u> are laws passed by the local
        legislative body.
    f) <u>Common law</u> - see above.

IV. Criminal Law and Civil Law:
    a) <u>Criminal law</u> are the laws of crime and their
        punishment - e.g. murder, rape, assault,
        battery, etc.

b) <u>Civil law</u> is all law that is not criminal. It is the law of private rights developed from ancient Roman law.

V. Contracts:
    a) A <u>contract</u> is a legally enforceable agreement between two or more parties.
        1. In order for a contract to exist there must be an offer and an acceptance.
        2. For a contract to be valid, four elements for a contract have to be considered valid by the courts.
            a. <u>Mutual assent</u> - both parties to the contract must understand what they are agreeing to. There cannot be any fraud, any duress or undue influence.
            b. <u>Consideration</u> is something of value which is exchanged between the parties entering into a contract. This "something of value" can be either money, goods or services or a combination of the three. If there isn't "something of value" exchanged, there isn't a valid contract.
            c. <u>Contractual capacity</u> means the legal ability of all parties to enter into a contract. For example, a person must be of legal age and be considered mentally competent to enter into a contract.

           d. Legal purpose – in order
               for the courts to en-
               force a contract, the
               contract must not be
               for the purpose of
               committing an illegal
               act. For example,
               entering into a con-
               tract to open a house
               of prostitution in
               New York state will
               not be enforced by
               the courts.

VI. Remedies at law for a breach (broken) of contract:
     a) There are four remedies at law for a breach of
         contract.
               1. Damages can be paid to the wronged
                   party if a contract is broken.
                   The court determines if and how
                   much damages should be paid.
               2. Specific performance is when the
                   wronged party might ask the
                   court to order that the contract
                   be fulfilled as originally agreed.
                   For example, if a contract was
                   made to sell a house and the
                   owner later refused to sell it,
                   the court may order that the
                   original contract be carried out.
               3. Injunction is a court order that
                   prohibits a particular activity
                   from occurring. For example,
                   an illegal strike takes place and
                   the court orders the strikers to
                   cease and desist.
               4. Recission occurs when a court issues
                   an order to cancel, or rescind,
                   a contract. This usually occurs
                   when one party has misled the
                   other.

VII. Uniform Commercial Code (U.C.C.) – 1952
      a) The Uniform Commercial Code was passed in
          order to create a uniformity of regulation
          among the states. Until this code was pass-
          ed it was almost impossible to participate in
          interstate commerce.

1. The provisions of the Uniform Commercial Code set uniform laws in all states for business activities involving such items as bills of lading, stock transfers, negotiable instruments, etc.
2. The U.C.C. makes it possible to do business between people and/or businesses from different states without concerning oneself that the laws are not uniform.

VIII. Key legal terms:
   a) Garnishment - the employer of the defendant is ordered by the court to withhold a certain amount of money from the employee's earnings until the judgement against the defendant is satisfied.
   b) Agency occurs when one party, the principal, gives authorization to another person, who becomes the agent, to represent the principal in conducting various types of business activities. Some examples of an agent are: stockbrokers, waiters and sales clerks.
      1. Power of attorney is written authorization given by a principal to an agent to act in the principal's behalf.
      2. Any contract entered into by the agent on behalf of the principal is binding on the principal. However, if the agent acts illegally or outside what he was authorized to act by the principal, the agent can be held libel for damages by the principal.
   c) Property is legally classified as being anything of value by which a person, business or other group has the sole right of ownership. Examples of property is an automobile, a suit, a house, land, jewelry, etc.
      1. Tangible real property is land or anything attached to the land. For example, a house or appliance in the house are tangible real property.

2. Tangible personal property are move-
able items such as clothing and
jewelry. These items can either
be bought, sold, leased or owned.
3. Intangible personal property are such
items as stock certificates, insurance policies and bank accounts.
These items have written docu-
mentation but they cannot be
seen.

d) Deed - is a written cotnract that transfers the
ownership of real property.

e) Title is the legal ownership and the right to use
the property. Title usually takes the form
of a document that serves as proof of ownership of the property.

f) Warranty - is a promise made by a seller that
the product or service will be or perform as
represented. For example, the seller stating
that the power train of an automobile will
last for five years.

g) Express warranty - contains factual statements
about the quality of the property sold. The
house had aluminum siding put on it last
year; is an example of an express warranty.

h) Copyright is the right to control the reproduc-
tion and distribution of creative works. For
example, most publishers have copyrights of
their publication.

i) Patent - is an exclusive legal right to a particular product.

j) Negotiable instruments are written contractual
obligations used mainly in business activities.
Examples of negotiable instruments are checks
and promissory notes.

k) Endorsement is the common method of transferring a negotiable instrument. When a person
signs the back of a check, he is endorsing
the check.
1. Blank endorsement - no restrictions
are placed on how the check is
used. The one who is paid only
has to sign his or her name on
the back of the check.
2. Restrictive endorsement - limits the
transferring of a negotiable
instrument - e.g. writing "for
deposit only" on the back of a
check.

3. Special endorsement identifies the specific person to whom the check is to be paid - e.g. "pay to the order of Stephen R. Smith."

4. Qualified endorsement shows that the endorser of the check does not guarantee payment of the check if the account of the payer has insufficient funds. This is signed "without recourse."

1) Trademark - is a name or a symbol or other means of identification that has been officially registered with the government by the owner or producer as a means of identifying his product.

IX. Torts:

a) A tort is a noncriminal (civil) act that causes injury to another person or his property.

1. Intentional torts are:

a. Libel - a written or oral defamatory statement that conveys an unfair unfavorable impression.

b. Fraud - an act of deceit and/or misrepresentation.

c. Slander - the speaking of false charges that harms another's reputation.

d. Trespass - is to enter the land of another against the other person's will.

e. Assault - is the threat to do a violent act to another without the actual committing of the act.

f. Battery - is the actual committing of the violent act such as actually punching someone in the nose.

2. An unintentional tort is when another person or his property is harmed without it being done on purpose. When one is negligent, it implies carelessness, inattentiveness, lack of proper care

and inattention to one's responsibility. For example, if you buy a TV set, bring it home, plug it in, turn it on, and it explodes, the store from which you bought the set is most likely legally responsible to replace the set and repair all damages to property or persons.

    3. Product liability is a type of tort in which a firm is liable for any harm their product or service caused. This can be either intentional or result from negligence.

        a. Strict product liability is a type of tort in which a firm is held to be liable for any damage caused by a product it produces or markets. They are still held liable even if there was no deliberate tort or negligence involved.

X. BANKRUPTCY LAW

    a) Bankruptcy occurs when debtors who cannot meet their financial obligations to their creditors, have their assets split up among the creditors. Bankruptcy is a legal process and therefore, it is administered by the court system.

        1. Bankruptcy proceedings can be either voluntary or involuntary.

            a. Voluntary bankruptcy is when the debtor initates the process himself. This is usually the case when the debtor's liabilities is greater than his assets.

            b. Involuntary bankruptcy is when the creditors initiate bankruptcy proceedings in an

attempt to collect
some of the money
owed to them by the
debtor.

2. When a business is liquidated by the
bankruptcy court, all the debt-
or's assets are sold and the
proceeds of the sale are divided
among the various creditors.
This is known as Chapter 7.
However, one should be aware
that in many cases the debtor
has so little assets, that the
creditors receive next to nothing from the liquidation sale.
In many cases, the creditors get
together with the debtor and
work out a system of payments.
They will do this even if they
feel that they will not get all
their money back. In many in-
stances they believe that they
will do better this way than by
having to force the debtor to
go into the bankruptcy court
and have his business liquidated.

3. In some cases the bankruptcy court
will take the position that the
debtor will be able to pay off
his debts in the future. The
court will then appoint a trustee
to take control of the business,
and reorganize it in the hope of
making it profitable once more.
While this is occurring, the
bankruptcy court will protect
the debtor from the creditors'
payment demands. This is
known as the business being in
Chapter 11.

4. Bankruptcy is the final act for
settling the financial obligations
between debtors and their creditors. In the legal process of
bankruptcy, the debtor is re-
leased from his financial obligations to his creditors.

5. Congress has the authority to establish bankruptcy laws for the entire nation as per Article I, Section 8 of the U. S. Constitution.
   a. Bankruptcy Reform Act of 1978 was passed by the U. S. Congress in the hope that creditors will be treated fairly and that the debtors will be able to begin again without any encumberances. However, many creditors feel that this act is more beneficial to the debtor than to themselves.

QUESTIONS FOR REVIEW AND DISCUSSION

1. Describe the different types of law?

2. How is criminal law different from civil law?

3. Explain the necessary clauses that a valid contract must have.

4. Why was the passing of the Uniform Commercial Code important to trade and commerce in The United States?

5. How can a contract be breeched?

6. Discuss the remedies at law for dealing with a breach of contract.

7. How is involuntary bankruptcy different from voluntary bankruptcy?

8. Do the bankruptcy laws favor the debtor or the creditor? Discuss.

VI
SOCIAL AND ETHICAL RESPONSIBILITY IN BUSINESS

I.   a) Beginning in the last half of the twentieth century there has been greater attention by U. S. business to its various social and ethical responsibilities. Most Americans believe that social responsibility is a duty of business. At the very least, most believe that a business should not harm the welfare of society. A business that pollutes the environment, makes products that are unsafe, and displays a disregard for the society is deemed to be socially irresponsible.

           One can contend that there is an implied social contract between society and the business organization. Since society allows the business firm to exist, the business firm has the responsibility to act in a socially responsible and ethical manner. Social responsibility and ethical behavior is also considered by many to be good for business since it also encourages the public to have positive feelings about the company.

      b) However, there are some who believe that social responsibility is not a concern of business.

           1. <u>Milton Friedman</u> has stated that social responsibility is not a major concern of business.

                  a. Friedman stated that the prime responsibility of business management is the stockholders. He contends that the stockholders are entitled to the profits of the business and if the management gives money away to social causes it takes money away from the profits that the shareholders are entitled to. In addition, money is also taken away from increases in

43

wages that the
employees of the
company are also
entitled to.

2. Peter Drucker has taken the position
that it is imperative for business
to make a profit in order for it
to survive. Therefore, profitability should be the sole determination applied to all business
decisions.

c) For the great majority of American industrial
history, little attention was paid to the areas
of social responsibility business. Such areas
as black lung disease, the affect of asbestos,
the affect of insect sprays, dumping of waste
into bodies of water, air pollution due to the
release of smoke and chemicals into the at-
mosphere, pollution from automobiles, etc.,
were ignored by most segments of American
society.

However, certain tragedies such as acid
rain, disease and suffering from chemicals
and automobile accidents brought attention to
the problem of social and ethical responsibility of business.

In 1962 President John F. Kennedy
established a Consumer Advisory Council
which eventually published a "Bill of Rights"
for the consumer. These rights included:

1. The right to safety
2. The right to be informed
3. The right to choose
4. The right to be heard.

Kennedy's consumer interest led to such
consumer legislation in the 1960's as:

1. The Cigarette Labelling Act
2. The Fair Packing and Labeling
Act
3. The Truth in Advertising Act
4. The Truth in Lending Act
5. The Child Protection Act.

II. Government Regulation of Business:

a) The United States government has had a history
of regulating various aspects of business in
the country in order to facilitate competition
and maintain a free marketplace for all legal
kinds of business to flourish.

b) In order to maintain and promote open competition there has been a series of laws passed
by the federal government over the years.
1. The Sherman Act (1890) was the
first legislation aimed at regulating trusts. The object of the
Sherman Act was to prevent
illegal combinations restraining
trade. This act was against
such acts as boycotts and price
fixing.
The Sherman Act was basically an anti-monopoly law. However, because it was written in
such general language it was
difficult to enforce. For example, a Supreme Court Case such
as the E. C. Knight Case (1895)
made the Sherman Act difficult
to enforce.
2. Clayton Act (1913) was more specific
than the Sherman Act which
made it easier to enforce. The
Clayton Act specifically forbade
tying arrangements, exclusive
deals and mergers which had the
effect of significantly lessening
competition. Also forbidden by
the Clayton Act was interlocking
directorates in which one person
sat on the board of directors of
two or more firms dealing with
the same customers.
c) The Anti-trust (anti-monopoly) laws were established for the purpose of preserving free
and open competition and attempting to stop
one business from gaining a monopoly.
1. Monopoly - one business has the
power to set any prices it wishes
and can exclude other companies
from competing against it.
d) Federal Trade Commission Act (1914) - established the Federal Trade Commission with the
authority to deal with unfair trade practices.
e) The Robinson-Patman Act (1938) was established
to make competition more equitable. It forbade price discrimination which is the selling
of goods to different purchasers at different

prices by a commercial seller. However, this act is very difficult to enforce.

f) National Environmental Policy Act (1969) was established to assist the government in enforcing regulations in order to protect the environment from abuses of the air, water and other elements.

g) The United States government also may intervene in certain situations when business cannot make necessary items that some people in the society need; for example, pharmaceutical companies manufacture drugs for rare diseases. These companies are subsidized in part by the government.

    1. The government also regulated food and drug production. This power was established by The Pure Food and Drug Act (1906) and The Pure Cosmetic Act (1937).

    2. The government (federal, state, and local) also have regulated the workplace. This has been done by the passing of child labor laws, health codes in the workplace, safety controls and the setting up of government agencies such as the Occupational Safety and Health Administration (OSHA).

    3. At present the federal, state and many local governments are regulating such areas as the environment (e.g. acid rain, toxic waste, sewage disposal, etc.), food and drugs and occupational safety.

h) The United States is presently faced with the dilemma of how much regulation the government should have. If the government has too much regulation it could discourage people from going into business. If the government has too little regulation there is the danger of too many abuses.

However, in recent years there has been a move toward governmental deregulation. This has been done in part to encourage more Americans to enter business and to successfully compete against business from other nations.

QUESTIONS FOR REVIEW AND DISCUSSION

1. How much social responsibility does a business organization owe to the public?

2. Why has interest in social responsibility by a business organization grown?

3. Is it difficult to make a profit in a business and be ethical at the same time? Explain.

4. What do you think of the social responsibility philosophy of Milton Friedman and Peter Drucker?

5. How did the Sherman Act and the Clayton Act attempt to regulate business?

6. How much control should the U. S. government have over American business? Why?

VII

FORMS OF BUSINESS OWNERSHIP

I. The three basic forms of business ownership are sole proprietorships, partnerships and corporations.

    a) Sole proprietorship is a form of business ownership which is owned and operated by one individual. This person owns all the assets and is responsible for the debts of the business.

        1. The sole proprietorship is the most common form of private business ownership in the United States.

        2. It is commonly found in small retailing, service and farming businesses.

        3. Advantages of the sole proprietorship:

            a. Owner keeps all the profits.

            b. Formation of the business is easy.

            c. Dissolution of the business is easy.

            d. Tax advantages for owner.

            e. Decisions can be made quickly.

            f. Owner has a great deal of flexibility.

        4. Disadvantages of the sole proprietorship:

            a. Unlimited liability - the owner is alone responsible for any financial liability.

            b. Lack of capital.

            c. Lack of management skills - it is impossible for the sole proprietor to be an expert in everything.

            d. Lack of continuity.

　　　　　　　　　e.　The sole proprietor
　　　　　　　　　　　must make all the
　　　　　　　　　　　major decisions.
　b)　Partnership is an association of two or more peo-
　　　ple who operate as co-owners of a business
　　　by voluntary legal agreement.
　　　　　　1.　General partnership - are full owners
　　　　　　　　of a portion of the business and
　　　　　　　　share in all financial liabilities.
　　　　　　2.　Limited partnership - the partners
　　　　　　　　have liability limited up to the
　　　　　　　　amount of capital (money) they
　　　　　　　　have invested in the partnership.
　　　　　　3.　Joint Venture - is a temporary part-
　　　　　　　　nership formed for a specific
　　　　　　　　project (e.g. Alaska Pipeline),
　　　　　　　　in order to make a profit.
　　　　　　4.　Advantages of a partnership:
　　　　　　　　a.　Easy to form.
　　　　　　　　b.　Additional management skills
　　　　　　　　　　and specialization con-
　　　　　　　　　　tributed by the partners.
　　　　　　　　c.　Increased ability to raise
　　　　　　　　　　capital.
　　　　　　　　d.　Tax advantages.
　　　　　　　　e.　Limited regulation by govern-
　　　　　　　　　　ment.
　　　　　　5.　Disadvantages of a partnership:
　　　　　　　　a.　Unlimited liability - creditors
　　　　　　　　　　may have the owner's
　　　　　　　　　　personal possessions
　　　　　　　　　　attached if debts are not
　　　　　　　　　　paid by the business.
　　　　　　　　b.　Conflict among the partners.
　　　　　　　　c.　Lack of continuity.
　　　　　　　　d.　Difficulty in dissolving the
　　　　　　　　　　partnership if one part-
　　　　　　　　　　ner should decide to
　　　　　　　　　　leave the association.
　　　　　　6.　Steps in dissolving the partnership:
　　　　　　　　a.　Dissolution is the act where
　　　　　　　　　　at minimum, one of the
　　　　　　　　　　partners has terminated
　　　　　　　　　　the partnership associ-
　　　　　　　　　　ation.
　　　　　　　　b.　Liquidation is the act that
　　　　　　　　　　concludes the partner-
　　　　　　　　　　ship by paying its debts,

repaying capital contri-
butions to each of the
partners and dividing up
leftover funds.

    c. <u>Termination</u> is when the
liquidation is finished
and the partnership
association is concluded.

c) Corporation

According to U. S. Supreme Court Chief
Justice John Marshall who in 1819 stated, that
the corporation is "an artificial being, invisible,
intangible and existing only in contemplation of
the law." Therefore, the corporation is a "legal
person" existing under the laws of the particular
state in which it is created. Since the corporation is a "legal person," it can buy property,
enter into contracts, sue or be sued and it can
be taxed.

State approval is a requirement for a
corporate charter. The corporate charter spells
out the rights and privileges of the corporation.

The chief governing body of a corporation
is the board of directors. The board of directors is elected by the stockholders, who are the
owners of the corporation. Because the stockholders are the owners of the corporation and
elect the board of directors, the board is responsible to the stockholders.

One of the main concerns of the board of
directors is the appointment of the chief officers
of the corporation. The board of directors
appoint the chief executive officer (CEO) and
other executive officers of the corporation.

    1. <u>Advantages</u> of a corporation
        a. <u>Limited liability</u> - you
are only liable for
the investment in
the corporation.
Your personal wealth
is not liable.
        b. Specialized and expert
management skills.
        c. Economies of scale - the
more you produce
the cheaper the cost
per unit.
        d. Ease of raising capital.

                    e. Life of the corporation is
                        perpetual – if the
                        CEO dies or leaves,
                        the company still
                        goes on.
            2. Disadvantages of a corporation
                    a. Difficult and expensive
                        to form and dissolve
                        a corporation.
                    b. Tax disadvantage –
                        double taxation – the
                        corporation pays
                        taxes on the profits
                        and the stockholder
                        pays taxes on the
                        dividends.
                    c. More government restric-
                        tions.

QUESTIONS FOR REVIEW AND DISCUSSION

1. Explain the advantages and disadvantages of a sole pro-
    proprietorship.

2. Explain the advantages and disadvantages of a partnership.

3. Explain the advantages and disadvantages of a corporation.

4. Which factors determine the form of business that an
    organizer chooses?

5. Compare and contrast the owner's liability in the three
    major forms of business.

6. Which of the three major forms of business has the best
    chance of raising capital with which to start or expand
    the business? Why?

PART TWO

MANAGEMENT

VIII

MANAGEMENT

I. Management is the process of using people and other resources to achieve goals and objectives by coordinating available resources efficiently.
    a) Managers work with and through other people in getting the tasks accomplished in order to fulfill the objectives of the company.

II. There are four major functions in management:
    a) Planning is where the manager determines the goals of the firm and determines how future events will affect these goals. The manager must determine the type of activities necessary to see that the goals are achieved.
    b) Organizing is where the manager arranges the human resources, the physical resources, and sets up the various tasks needed to help the company achieve its objectives.
    c) Leading or Directing is where the manager guides people, motivates people and coordinates the various tasks and responsibilities of people in order to fulfill the objectives of the firm.
    d) Controlling is where the manager directs the process by which actual behavior or production is measured against established goals and objectives of the company. Actual performance is compared against established standards and corrective action is taken if it deemed necessary.

III. There are three levels of management:
    a) Top Management deals with the overall planning of the business such as long-range policy and strategy.
    b) Middle Management organizes and directs long-range plans which have been developed by top management. Middle management is in charge of the actual administration and operation of the company.
    c) Supervisory Management is directly in charge of carrying out the plans of middle management and are directly responsible for fulfilling the defined tasks done by employees who are not part of management.

IV. Management sets and carries out the policy of the company.
a) A <u>policy</u> is a statement of principle or a group of principles with certain rules that helps the company achieve its objectives.
b) Policy is developed by a combination of the social, economic and political forces within the society. Policy is also influenced by the ethics of society in general and business in particular.
c) The <u>main function of the business manager</u> is to help the firm produce its product and/or service as efficiently as possible and to provide the public with fair value at a price that will enable the company to make a competitive profit.

V. The successful business manager can help benefit American capitalism by:
1. Producing goods and services at a fair value.
2. Encouraging belief in private property and free competition.
3. Encouraging the belief that profit is the proper reward for successfully taking risks in business and providing goods and/or services for the customer at a fair price.
4. Believing in incentives, rewards and penalties in order to encourage progress.
5. Believing in high ethical standards as being most important in good business dealings.
6. Treating labor in a fair manner.
7. Encouraging research and development.
8. Encouraging individual initiative and freedom of inquiry.

VI. Scientific Management School:
a) The Scientific Management School deals with the application of scientific methods to business. These people see management as a system of mathematical models and processes and rely strongly on the application of scientific analysis to the problems of management. The scientific school believes that management is a process of interrelated functions. They believe that management principles are extremely important. They accept the position that there is a universality of management

whereas all managers do the same basic functions. Those who favor the Scientific
Management School are usually versed in
quantitative methods, computer technology
and systems analysis.

b) <u>Frederick W. Taylor</u> (1856-1915) is known as the
"father of scientific management."
1. Founded the "exception principle" -
   manager should schedule his
   workload so that subordinates
   handle the routine assignments
   while he devotes his time to
   exceptional problems and situations.
2. In his book <u>Principles of Scientific</u>
   <u>Management</u> (1911). Taylor said
   that managing is "knowing
   exactly what you want men to do,
   and then seeing that they do it
   in the best and cheapest way."
3. Labor and management should not
   argue about how profits would
   be divided but should concentrate on maximizing profits.
4. Taylor concentrated on the fiscal aspects of business but overlooked
   human nature.
5. Taylor believed "that the best
   management is a true science,
   resting upon clearly defined
   laws, rules, and principles, as
   a foundation."
6. Taylor favored scientifically selecting
   and then training the workers
   instead of letting them train
   themselves.
7. Taylor believed that responsibility
   and work should be divided
   equally among management and
   workers.

c) Frank (1868-1924) and Lillian (1878-1972)
   Gilbreth
1. Looked for "the one best way" to do
   a specific task through the
   method of motion study.
2. Lillian Gilbreth was one of the earli-
   est founders of what is presently
   known as personnel management.
   She believed in the scientific

56

selection, training and placement
of human resources.
3. The Gilbreths developed the merit-
rating system.

VII. Management Science School:
a) Sometimes known as the operations research (OR)
school.
b) This is the application of scientific methodology
in obtaining solutions to problems which developed in the operation of a system that
can be represented by a mathematical model,
and finding the solution to these problems
by using mathematical equations which represent the system.
c) This school had its start during World War II
when scientists were organized into research
groups to solve various operational problems
which the military faced. One of these
problems was in determining the correct number of ships needed to protect a convey as
it was crossing the Atlantic Ocean and the
size that the convoy should be in order to
receive the best protection.
d) The Scientific method included:
1. observe the system
2. build a model
3. observe the model to see how the system
would react
4. test the model.
e) The success of the operations research approach
was so, that by the mid-1950's management
science techniques were being applied to
such managerial problems as product packaging, location of plants and the scheduling
of production.
f) The Systems thinking approach to management:
1. Founded by Ludwig Von Bertalanffy.
2. The key idea of the general systems
theory is that a complete understanding of the whole operation of
an entity requires that it be viewed
as a complete system.
3. A system is an organized group of inter-
dependent parts, components or
subsystems joined together and functioning as a whole to achieve some
objective.

g) One basic benefit that management believes system theory gives, is <u>synergy</u> - that the sum of the product is greater than the sum of its individual parts.

h) The systems approach helps the manager to focus on how all segments of the organization are interrelated. Within the systems approach, the management system is generally open and interrelates with its environment. Among the environmental influences which the management system confronts is competition from other firms. Any or all of these influences can alter the future of a particular management system using "Systems Methodology."

QUESTIONS FOR REVIEW AND DISCUSSION

1. Describe the four major functions of management.

2. Explain the three levels of management.

3. How can a successful business manager benefit American capitalism?

4. Why is Frederick W. Taylor known as the "father of scientific management?"

5. How does the systems approach help the manager?

I. <u>Leadership</u> is the ability to get people to do what the leader wishes them to do. This can come about because the leader influences or inspires subordinates to achieve certain objectives.

    a) Types of leadership:

        John French, Jr. and Bertram Raven, in "The Bases of Social Power," in Cartwright, Dorwin and Zander (eds.), <u>Group Dynamics</u>, 2nd ed. (Evanston, Illinois: Row, Peterson & Co., 1960), 607-623 have described five main sources of leadership.

           1. <u>Coercive Power</u> - this is power based on fear. The fear can be either physical or psychological. Failure to comply with the desires of the superior will lead to punishment.

           2. <u>Reward Power</u> is opposite of coercive power. The subordinate believes that following the desires of the superior will result in a positive reward, either monetary (an increase in pay), or psychological (a compliment).

           3. <u>Legitimate Power</u> is acquired because of the manager's position within the organization. For example, the president of the company has more legitimate power than a department vice-president.

           4. <u>Expert Power</u> is acquired by an individual who has some special knowledge, skill or expertise which enables him to obtain the respect of peers and subordinates.

5. Referent Power is based on the subordinate's identification with the leader. The subordinates are influenced because of their admiration for the leader.

b) Six Types of Leadership Styles:

1. Autocratic leaders make decisions and give orders. They depend on the authority of their position to have subordinates follow them. Autocratic leaders give little or no credance to the opinions of their subordinates.

2. Democratic leaders communicate and seek out the opinion's of their subordinates. Decisions will most likely reflect the opinion of the group because the democratic leader accepts input from the group.

3. Laissez-faire (free-rein) leaders allows subordinates to make most of their own decisions. This kind of leader exercises little supervisory control and because of this, agreement in decision-making is often difficult to obtain.

4. Benevolent autocratic leaders are powerful but are sincerely concerned about the welfare of their subordinates.

5. Job-centered leaders concentrate on job structure. They closely supervise their subordinates so that they can complete all the necessary jobs.

6. Employee-centered leaders emphasize human relations and allow their subordinates to have a large amount of freedom in doing their work.

c) Contingency Theory of Leadership is based on the view that different leadership styles are more effective with different groups in different situations. Management action and style depend upon the

circumstances of the situation the manager faces.
1. The situation is determined by:
    a. the size of the organization
    b. the manager's relation with his subordinates
    c. the kind of job that must be performed.
2. Contingency Theory was founded by Fiedler, Fred E., A Theory of Leadership Effectiveness, New York: McGraw-Hill Co., 1967.
d) Douglas McGregor believed there are at least four variables involved in leadership:
    1. The characteristics of the leader.
    2. The attitudes and needs of the followers.
    3. The characteristics of the organization.
    4. The social, political and economic atmosphere.

QUESTIONS FOR REVIEW AND DISCUSSION

1. Explain the various types of leadership styles.

2. Is the Contingency Theory of Leadership a benefit to management? How?

3. Describe Douglas McGregor's four variables involved in leadership.

PLANNING, ORGANIZING AND CONTROLLING

I. <u>Planning</u> is the process of formulating objectives and determining courses of action in order to successfully achieve the objectives.

    a) Steps in the planning process:
1. Determine what has to be accomplished
2. Collect and organize the necessary information
3. Determine what kind of problems you may face
4. Determine what kind of actions you may take if you cannot solve various problems
5. Determine the type of plan you will follow in order to accomplish your objectives
6. Determine the methods of controlling the plan.

    b) Plans can be divided into three parts:
1. Time - determines how long the plan would be in effect
2. Use - determining the activities that are necessary for the plan to be carried out
3. Breadth - determining how much the plan should include.

    c) Planning should be flexible. Managers should be able to make adjustments when necessary so that the following questions are answered continually.
1. Where are we now?
2. Where are we going?
3. What problems are we facing?
4. Can we overcome these problems?
5. Are we moving in the right direction?
6. Will we get to where we want to be at the right time?

II. Advantages and Disadvantages of Planning:

	Advantages		Disadvantages
1.	Focuses attention on objectives.	1.	Information may be incorrect.
2.	Provides a basis for people in the firm to work as a team.	2.	Difficult to predict changes in the future.
3.	The firm is forced to adapt to its environment.	3.	Objectives may not have good co-ordination among various departments.
4.	Helps to anticipate problems.	4.	People may get tied to plans too much and this might reduce their ability and desire to maneuver when necessary.
5.	Provides direction in a firm's activities.		
6.	Helps to make the controlling function easier.		
7.	Provides alternatives to possible deviations in the plan.		

ORGANIZING

I. <u>Organizing</u> is a meaningful function which determines:
   a) the various jobs to be done
   b) putting particula<u>r</u> jobs into departments
   c) relations betwee<u>n</u> various departments
   d) coordinating all aspects of the organization.

II. <u>Organizational structures</u> are the order and responsibility of various types of relationships between the
   employees, the job, and departments within the company. These relationships are made up of human
   resources, physical resources, informational resources
   and financial resources.

III. Differences between formal and informal organizations:
   a) <u>Formal organization</u> - is the organizational chart
      which shows the formal authority relation-
      ships between superiors and subordinates
      within the organization.
   b) <u>Informal organization</u> - are the various working
      relationships, friendships, coffee klatches,
      social groups and other relationships that
      effect the work of the firm. The informal
      group leader emerges from within the group
      and is usually able to provide leadership
      for the group.

IV. Differences between Line, Staff and Functional authority
   within the organization:
   a) <u>Line authority</u> - is the authority which re-
      lates directly to the activities necessary
      to the accomplishment of the firm's ob-
      jectives. For example, in a textile
      manufacturing firm, the production of
      the fabric and the sale of the fabric are
      line activities. A <u>line organization</u> is
      one in which direct authority flows down-
      ward from the top levels of management
      to the lower management levels.
   b) <u>Staff authority</u> - deals with those who are
      not directly related to achieving the ob-
      jectives of the organization. They give
      advice and serve as consultant to vari-
      ous units of the organization. For exam-
      ple, in a textile manufacturing firm, the
      textile engineer has staff authority.

c) Functional authority - is similar to line authority but it cuts across organizational
lines in a specific area. For example,
the personnel manager may have a say of
who gets hired within any department.

d)

Advantages	Disadvantages

Line Authority

Advantages	Disadvantages
1. It is simple	1. Lacks special-ists
2. It is fast	
3. Responsibility is known	2. Overworks some people
4. Clear chain-of-command distribu-tion of authority and re-sponsibil-ity on all levels	3. Depends on certain key people
	4. Delays can be caused if line manag-ers wait for staff input before acting, causing a slowdown in produc-tivity.
5. Unity of Com-mand - each per-son in the chain of command has only one super-visor to whom he or she is ac-countable.	

Staff Authority

Advantages	Disadvantages
1. Expert advise is received from spe-cialists	1. Not always clear who is re-sponsible
2. Line executives can consult for another opinion.	2. Another level of bureau-cracy has to be over-come for some ac-tivity to occur.

Functional Authority

1. One knowledgeable in a specific function makes the decisions. 2. If set-up correctly, authority is simplified.	1. Difficulty in determining which executive has authority 2. Problem of determining responsibility 3. Jealously among executives 4. Can undermine the authority of the manager in the product division.

III. Relationship between Authority and Responsibility:
   a) Authority is the right to act or make decisions within certain limits.
   b) Responsibility is a person's duty to perform an assigned task or job.
   c) Delegation is the giving of some authority to a subordinate along with the responsibility for doing a specific job.
   d) Accountability is a person's liability for performing assigned tasks.
   e) Span of Control is the optimum number of people a manager can supervise in an effective manner.

IV. Committee organization is made up of various groups of individuals who share authority and responsibility. These groups are usually formed for specific purposes such as developing a new product, new research, brainstorming, etc. Committee organizations often represent large areas of the organization such as marketing, finance and manufacturing. These committees provide people from various parts of the firm to meet together and work on solving a specific problem.

V. Quality Circles are voluntary groups of employees who meet to solve specific problems in the firm. They are made up of employees who do similar work. Management receives proposed solutions from each of the quality circles that are organized. It is hoped by management, that quality circles will serve to motivate employees to have more interest in their job and the welfare of the firm as a whole.

VI.   <u>Departmentalization</u> is the grouping of job activities and functions into organizational units. The organizational units should be related and specific.
    a)   Types of Departmentalization:
        1.   <u>Functional Departmentalization</u> – groups workers according to their job function; e.g. marketing, production, accounting, etc.
        2.   <u>Product Departmentalization</u> is grouping according to specific product lines. Each group is responsible for all aspects of the product whether it is manufacturing or marketing the product.
        3.   <u>Geographical Departmentalization</u> is the grouping of the company's product and service by location.
        4.   <u>Customer Departmentalization</u> is based on the grouping of customers who have special requirements or characteristics.

VII.   Centralized vs. Decentralized Authority
    1.   <u>Centralized Authority</u> is when the majority of decision-making authority and responsibility remains within the levels of upper-management.
    2.   <u>Decentralized Authority</u> is when a great deal of authority and responsibility is assigned to middle and supervisory (lower) management, e.g. General Motors, Chrysler and other American automobile manufacturers are highly decentralized.
    3.   Advantages of Centralized and Decentralized organizational authority:

Centralized	Decentralized
1. Greater direct control to manager with most knowledge to make decisions	1. Subordinates can develop the confidence and ability to make decisions

2. Manager has full responsibility for the decisions.	2. Firm will benefit because subordinates will be able to move up within the firm and replace vacancies in higher-level management. 3. Control is facilitated.

VIII. Functional Organizational Structure:
   a) The functional organizational structure is defined as one in which there are a number of functional specialists who are responsible for supervising the activities of a single worker.
      1. Different staff departments have line authority over the particular worker.
      2. The worker and/or subordinate is accountable to all of the functional specialists.
   b) The basic idea of the functional organization was begun by Frederick W. Taylor. Taylor believed that the conventional industrial foreman had so many duties that one person could not do all these satisfactorily. Therefore, he developed a structure in which each worker reported to eight foremen.
   c) Advantages and Disadvantages of Functional Organization:

Advantages	Disadvantages
1. Permits high degree of specialization	1. Authority and responsibility come into conflict.
2. Easier to fill positions because functional specialists need limited talents	2. At times very difficult to get specialized experts to work together in a cooperative manner.

68

3. People can be-
   come expert
   in their
   particular
   field
4. Provides better
   specialized
   supervision.

3. Violates the
   principle of
   a person
   being re-
   sponsible
   to a single
   authority
4. Very difficult
   for a com-
   pany to
   run smooth-
   ly when an
   individual
   is account-
   able to
   more than
   one person.

IX. What is controlling?
   a) <u>Controlling</u> is the process by which managers
      can compare performance against previously
      defined objectives to determine if objectives
      are being met.
   b) The three basic steps in the controlling process
      are:
      1. Setting standards
      2. Comparing results against the pre-
         determined standards
      3. Making corrections if there is any
         deviation from the standards.
   c) It is important to note that feedback is necessary
      to maintain control. Without feedback there
      cannot be any control.
   d) Controlling achieves its objectives by:
      1. Preventing some deviations before they
         occur
      2. Correcting deviations as they occur.

X. Controlling is important because:
   a) Helps firm to maintain standards of performance
   b) Holds various members of firm accountable for
      their performance
   c) Helps to detect changes as they are occurring
      and determine if the changes are desirable
   d) Helps to safeguard the firm's assets
   e) Helps to standardize performance
   f) Helps to motivate management and other employees
   g) Helps to make decentralization of control easier.

XI. What should an effective control system possess?
    a) Information that is useful and understandable
    b) Time conscious in that deviations are found quickly
    c) Flexibility to deal with varying situations and maintain control
    d) A method which helps provide correction action instead of just discovering errors.

XII. Financial Statements
    a) <u>Financial statements</u> are an organized collection of data which are developed according to consistent and logical methods of accounting.
    b) The objective of the financial statement is to show an understanding of the various financial aspects of the company.
    c) More about financial statements and other methods of controlling is found in the chapter on accounting.

QUESTIONS FOR REVIEW AND DISCUSSION

1. Explain the advantages and disadvantages of planning as it pertains to management.

2. How is Line, Staff and Functional Authority different? Which one do you favor?

3. Explain the advantages of Centralized and Decentralized organizational authority.

4. Discuss the advantages and disadvantages of functional organizational structure.

5. Why is controlling important?

6. What should an effective control system possess?

MOTIVATION

I.   What is Motivation?
    a)   Motivation is a person's inner state which causes that person to act in such a way that strives for the accomplishment of some objective.
    b)   Motivation helps to explain why people act the way they do.
    c)   It is important for managers to realize how to motivate people. Good motivators can achieve a great deal through people. If a manager realizes the needs of a member of the firm, he can then do what is necessary to help that person fulfill his needs.
        1.   Motivating members of the firm is the process of giving them the chance to satisfy their needs by performing in a satisfactory manner within the firm.
        2.   A member of the firm who is not finding his or her needs satisfied, may contribute towards the objectives of the firm in a negative way.
        3.   Managers who are considered to be good motivators stress the positive aspects of a subordinate's actions instead of stressing the negative aspects of that person's actions.

II. Various management strategies involved in motivating subordinates:
    a)   Good communication - subordinates who feel that they can talk to their superiors about various problems that they are confronted with, usually perform in a better fashion than if they cannot communicate in a positive way with the manager.
    b)   Positive attitude towards subordinates - those managers who believe that their subordinates can and do make positive contributions to the success of the firm, help to motivate their subordinates to do a good job. A manager's attitude towards those under him comes through to

the subordinates and affects their performance in either a positive or negative way, depending upon the attitude of the manager.

c) <u>Design of job</u> – how a manager designs a job for a specific individual has a large determination upon whether that individual does a good job.

d) <u>Job rotation</u> – at times it is better to move people from one type of job to another to prevent them from getting bored. Many people feel that job rotation will increase productivity.

e) <u>Job enlargement</u> – at times this strategy helps a worker perform in a more satisfactory manner by giving him more tasks of the job, many workers feel that they are advancing themselves within the organization and therefore become more productive.

f) <u>Flexitime</u> – this motivates some workers because they are allowed to arrange the type of hours that they desire within certain parameters of the firm.

III. Theories of Individual Behavior
    A. Maslow's hierarchy of human needs.

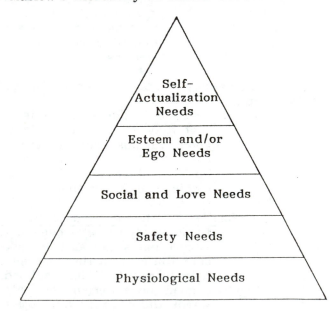

From lowest to the highest needs
1. Physiological needs - the need
    for food, clothing and shel-
    ter. These needs come before
    any other needs.
2. Safety needs - the need for
    safety, security and protec-
    tion.
3. Social and Love needs - man is a
    social animal. He needs to
    feel wanted and loved by
    other people and the feeling
    of belonging to a group.
4. Esteem and Ego needs - the need
    for a high opinion of oneself.
    This is also the need to have
    respect and be held in esteem
    by others.
5. Self-actualization needs - the
    necessity of a person to
    achieve their potential. This
    person is usually secure, self-
    confident, willing to learn
    from others and is willing to
    become close and have faith
    and trust in other people.
Maslow's theory gives managers the
    knowledge that money is not the only
    motivating force in getting subordi-
    nates to improve productivity. There
    are other needs, and the more a
    manager is aware of the other needs,
    the more effective he will be.

B. Kurt Lewin (1890-1947) and his field theory
    1. Lewin believed that behavior of a person
        is strongly influenced by his envir-
        ronment.
    2. Lewin's main work was A Dynamic Theo-
        ry of Personality (1935).

3. Field Theory

$$B = f(PE)$$

B=behavior
f=function of factors
P=Person
E=Environment

Behavior = function of the factors of
the person and the factors of the
environment as they have an effect upon that person.

C. David McClelland categorized three basic needs.
1. <u>Need for achievement</u> - the inner drive
to achieve success.
2. <u>Need for affiliation</u> - the wish to have
close interpersonal relations with
other people.
3. <u>Need for power</u> - the desire to feel able
to alter events and influence other
people. They strive to reach the
higher levels of power and influence
in an organization.

D. Carl Rogers
1. Main work was <u>On Becoming a Person</u>
(1961).
2. By studying all aspects of a person's
self-concept, one can understand
and even predict with a large degree
of accuracy, his mode of behavior.
3. Rogers strongly believed that a person's
environment strongly influenced his
self-concept.

E. B. F. Skinner
1. Skinner's main work was <u>The Behavior
of Organisms</u> (1938).
2. Derived the theory of "operant behavior,"
in which he states that behavior is
the result of various consequences.
3. Human behavior can be influenced by
other people if they know what
stimulus affects the person.
4. Skinner emphasized the importance of
reinforcement on voluntary behavior.

F. Douglas McGregor
  1. His chief work was <u>The Human Side of</u>
      <u>Enterprise</u> (1960).
  2. Theory X and Theory Y.

Theory X	Theory Y
(1) People do not like to work and will do all that they can do to avoid it.	(1) Work is a natural act for the average worker.
(2) They do not have a sense of responsibility.	(2) Under proper conditions the average worker will seek work.
(3) They have little ambition.	(3) Workers will exercise self-direction and self-control to achieve objectives.
(4) The average worker is self-centered and does not care about the firm's goals.	(4) If workers are committed to a firm's objectives they will be self-motivated.
(5) The average worker resists any change.	(5) Workers have the ability for creativity and ingenuity in finding solutions for various problems that the firm encounters.
(6) The average worker wants job security and economic security above all else.	

(7) To get the
average
worker
to achieve
the firm's
objectives,
it is nec-
essary to
use force,
control
and threats
of punish-
ment.

(6) Workers are
also inter-
ested in
satisfying
esteem and
self-actu-
alization
needs.

(7) For the aver-
age work-
er, secur-
ity is
important
but it is
not the
workers
only con-
sideration.

G. Chris Argyris
  1. Immaturity-Maturity Theory
    a) This theory outlines a number of
changes that occur as a per-
son moves from immaturity to
maturity such as activity,
depth of interest, etc.
    b) Argyris comes to the conclusion
that most firms keep their
employees in a perpetual
state of immaturity by discouraging mature behavior.

H. Victor Vroom
  1. Expectancy Theory that was put forward
by Vroom, means the probability that
a specific action will be followed by
highly probable and valuable rewards, which in turn will lead to a
large degree of job satisfaction if the
rewards are considered to be equitable.

I. Elton Mayo
  1. The Hawthorne Studies were conducted
by Mayo at the Western Electric
Corporation in a suburb of Chicago
between 1927 and 1932. The research showed a connection between
the workers morale and productivity.

The human relations school of management was based a great deal on the Hawthorne Studies.
2. The Hawthorne Studies under Elton Mayo came to the conclusion that better treatment of workers would increase their productivity.
3. Mayo came to the conclusion that improved productivity in both the controlled and experimental groups was because both groups received special attention from management.

J. Frederick Herzberg
1. Herzberg's main work was written with B. Mausner and B. Snyderman and called <u>The Motivation to Work</u> (1959).
2. Herzberg's <u>Two Factor Theory</u> consists of hygiene factors and motivational factors.

<u>Hygiene Factors</u>	<u>Motivational Factors</u>
(are things that would lead to job dissatisfaction).	(are things that will encourage people to achieve the firm's objectives and lead to job satisfaction).
(1) money	(1) achievement
(2) status	(2) recognition
(3) security	(3) responsibility
(4) working conditions	(4) personal growth
(5) relations with supervisors, peers and subordinates.	(5) chance for advancement.

K. There are many aspects that the manager has to consider in motivating employees. Money, of course, is very important. It is especially important when the employee receives a low wage and any decent increase in money will greatly increase the worker's productivity. However, money will not be so important if the employee is making a decent income and is interested in other things such as self-esteem, self-actualization, status, and respect.

    1. The manager should be aware that not only money but psychological factors such as achievement, recognition, advancement and responsibility are also successful motivational factors in increasing productivity.

    2. Each manager has to develop his own theory of motivation. However, most new managers feel that not only must they satisfy lower level needs of workers such as physiological and safety needs; but understands that many workers also feel the need to satisfy higher needs such as social, esteem and self-actualization needs.

    3. In general, various theories and research are of value in helping managers develop a philosophy of how to motivate subordinates. Managers should make their objectives clear; consider objections in a sincere and fair manner and respect the views of the subordinates at all times.

QUESTIONS FOR REVIEW AND DISCUSSION

1. What is motivation?

2. Why is it important to understand motivation in order to understand the role of leadership?

3. Explain Maslow's hierarchy of needs.

   a) Which need do you consider the most important? Why?

4. Can most people attain self-actualization? Give reasons for your answer.

5. Discuss the various strategies in motivating subordinates.

   a) Which strategy is the best? Why?

   b) Which strategy is the worst? Why?

6. Explain McClelland's three basic needs.

7. How can environment affect a person's behavior?

8. How does "Theory X" differ from "Theory Y"?

   a) Which theory do you think is correct? Why?

9. How did "The Hawthorne Studies" affect ideas on productivity?

10. Why is Herzberg's "Hygiene-Motivation Theory" useful?

11. What is the best position to assume in motivating people at work?

XII

MANAGEMENT OF HUMAN RESOURCES

I. Why is human resources management important?
    a) The key element of an organization is the people who work for that group.
        1. The organization runs on how the workers carry out their assigned functions in order to achieve the organization's objectives.
        2. Matching the correct person with the correct job is a vital function of the human resources department.
            a. The correct people are usually found within the firm.
            b. Human resource departments sometimes have to go outside the company.

II. Planning in the area of human resources:
    a) Planners have to determine what type of employees the firm needs and how many of each kind are necessary.

III. The process of selection:
    a) It must be generally understood that larger firms in most cases use more complex selection methods than smaller firms.
    b) Selection methods for upper-level management and technical staff jobs are generally much more complicated than the procedures for lower-level jobs.
    c) Various steps in the selection process:
        1. Recruitment
        2. Application
        3. Preliminary screening of applicants
        4. Testing
        5. Check of references
        6. Final interview
        7. Evaluation.

IV. Governmental influences:
    a) The Civil Rights Act - passed in 1964 and expanded in 1972 prohibits discrimination in all types of personnel practices and policies, such as recruitment, interviewing, testing,

compensation, promotion, union-management relations, and different kinds of treatment based on race, color, religion, sex or country of national origin.

b) The <u>Civil Rights Act</u> is enforced by the Equal Employment Opportunity Commission (EEOC).

c) <u>Affirmative Action</u> programs have been developed with the desire to increase job opportunities for minorities and women.

V. Training and Development

    a) <u>Orientation</u> is the introduction of new employees or those recently moved to a different job to the newer aspects of their new job.

        1. All orientation programs should include:

            a. the firm's background

            b. introduction to coworkers

            c. various aspects of the new worker's job

            d. company policies

            e. company benefits.

    b) <u>On-the-Job Training</u> (OJT) is to teach the employee how to do the job while he is on the job. This is usually done under the supervision of an experienced and productive worker. On-the-Job training should include:

        1. Planning.

        2. Preparing the worker.

        3. Showing the worker the methods and various operations of the job.

        4. Observing the worker at his new job and making suggestions as necessary.

        5. Follow-up and evaluation.

VI. Management Development:

    a) Management development training usually includes many activities and a variety of experiences.

        1. Types of Development

            a. On-the-Job training for managers. They learn how to manage by managing.

            b. Classroom attendance.

            c. Formal guidance from a supervisory manager, known as coaching.

       d. Seminars - both formal and
             informal.
       e. Staff meetings.
       f. Role playing - used in de-
             veloping human relations
             skills.
       g. Management games - people
             are put on teams and
             compete against each
             other.
       h. Sensitivity training - this is
             to develop realization of
             the effect of your actions
             on other people.
       i. Job-rotation - a manager can
             learn various things
             about the organization by
             moving from one job to
             another.
       j. Attend courses at local
             colleges.
       k. Self-development.

VII. Performance Review:
    a) During a performance review the manager and
        the subordinate should discuss the quality
        of the subordinate's performance; ways to
        improve; problems that they face; and what
        can be done in the future.
    b) Some methods of performance review are:
        1. Rating scales.
        2. Management-by-objectives (MBO) forms.
             This will be discussed later in the
             chapter.
        3. Follow-up of the performance-review.
            a. During this period of time the
               subordinate is observed to
               form the basis of discussion
               for the next performance
               review.
        4. The great jackass fallacy.
            a. This means that subordinates
               know the difference between
               being positively motivated by
               managers and being manip-
               ulated and therefore are not
               fooled by managers who are

insincere and try to manip-
ulate the subordinates via a
"carrot and stick" type reward system.

VIII.   Compensation and employee benefits:
a) Job evaluation - determines the salary level for
various jobs by determining the nature of
the job, the degree of responsibility involved
on each job, the amount of education needed
and the physical nature and risk involved.
By comparing one job with another job within the firm a relative degree of comparable
worth may be determined. However, one
should understand that a job that is worth a
particular amount to one company may be
valued differently by another company.
b) Direct monetary compensation.
1. Wages or salary - the actual amount of
money being paid to perform a specific job.
2. Bonuses - some companies have plans
that specifies if an individual performs successfully a specific amount
of work, that individual will receive
extra compensation.
3. Profit sharing - if the firm makes a
profit this is shared with the employees.
4. Stock sharing.
c) Indirect compensation.
This is called fringe benefits and is made up
of:
Retirement plans.
Health plans, e.g. medical and dental plans.
Life insurance plans.
Sick leave.
Vacations and holidays.

IX.   Promotion, transfers and separations.
a) Promotions - can be based on an employee's
merit, seniority, ability and sometimes nepo-
tism and political connections.
b) Transfers - movement from one part of the company to another job within the company.
This is usually called a lateral move that
may be brought about because of differences
between the worker and his superior or due

to boredom or a deterioration of relations between one worker and another.
c) Separations are made up of:
   1. Resignation - voluntary leaving of firm
      by employee.
   2. Layoffs - temporarily putting worker off
      job due to bad business times or
      plant conversion or the closing or
      moving of physical facilities.
   3. Dismissals - a person being fired normal-
      ly for poor performance but not al-
      ways the case.
   4. Retirements - after working for a spe-
      cific number of years an employee
      leaves with hopefully a sufficient
      pension.

X. Management by Objectives (MBO)
   a) MBO was popualrized by Peter Drucker in the
      1930's.
   b) MBO is sometimes called "Management by Re-
      sults."
   c) Under MBO, attention is directed on what should
      be accomplished rather than by the method-
      ology or how something will be accomplished.
   d) The steps in Management by Objectives
      1. Individual develops description of his or
         her objectives.
      2. Discussion between the individual and
         his or her superior in which short-
         term objectives (usually three months)
         are established.
      3. After short-term period, subordinate and
         superior get together to review ob-
         jectives and make revisions in the
         objectives if they both agree it is
         necessary.
      4. At various points under MBO the sub-
         ordinate and the superior meet regu-
         larly to go over the objectives and
         continue to make changes as neces-
         sary.
      5. At established periods, checks are made
         to establish if there is successful
         progress towards achieving the ob-
         jectives that were set.
      6. At the end of the period, the subordi-
         nate and superior meet to evaluate
         the efforts of the subordinate.

Reasons for goals being achieved or
not being achieved are discussed.
e) Advantages of MBO
   1. Agreement between superior and subordinate on the objectives to be
accomplished.
   2. Subordinate is encouraged to be responsible for his or her own decisions.
   3. Subordinate knows what is expected of
them.
   4. Subordinate knows the limits of what
they can or can't do.
   5. Morale may be improved because of the
subordinate having a say in what is
to be accomplished.
   6. Performance is evaluated by what is
accomplished instead of how one fol-
lows orders.
   7. The subordinate gets some freedom to
use their own ideas in accomplishing
their objectives.
f) Disadvantages of MBO
   1. Many managers are not committed to
MBO.
   2. Increases pressure on the individual
without giving him many choices of
objectives.
   3. MBO emphasizes the quantitative rather
than the qualitative in judging the
achievement of objectives.
   4. Top management usually does not support MBO and if they do they support it in a lukewarm manner.
   5. Many MBO programs just go through the
motions without any real results.
   6. Too much emphasis on paperwork in
order to justify MBO.
   7. The subordinate receives little help in
accomplishing the objectives.
   8. Qualitative work is not emphasized.
   9. Certain subordinates are not able to
work under an MBO system and
therefore should not be subjected
to it.
  10. Many managers do not know how to
implement a successful MBO program.

XI. Communication:
   a) Managers should understand the importance of communication. Good communication is important for successful managerial functioning. It is extremely important for managers to get their ideas across to subordinates and for their peers. If people do not understand the manager's thought, it is virtually impossible to achieve the various objectives of the firm.
   b) What is communication?
      1. Communication is the process of the interchange of information and thoughts between two or more people.
      2. Communication has the purpose of:
         a. Inquiring
         b. Informing
         c. Persuading.
      3. Communication skills
         a. Speaking
         b. Reading
         c. Writing
         d. Body language.
   c) Barriers to communication:
      1. Noise
      2. Emotions
      3. Language
      4. Lack of information
      5. Beliefs
      6. Poor channels
      7. Inappropriate timing
      8. Misperception
      9. Using words that have multimeaning
      10. Lack of attention
      11. Omission of details
      12. At times, too much information.
   d) Keys to effective communication:
      1. Be clear
      2. Be concise
      3. Be aware of the physical and emotional atmosphere while communicating
      4. Be positive whenever possible
      5. Be careful of the timing of the communication
      6. Be a good listener
      7. Be careful
      8. Follow-up.

e) Channels of communication:
    1. Formal channels
        a. Approved by the organization
        b. Recognized methods of communi-
            cation within the organi-
            zation.
    2. Informal channels
        a. These are channels outside the
            approved channels within the
            company. This is known as
            the grapevine.
        b. Management should be aware of
            the grapevine and try to use
            it as effectively as possible.
f) Effective communication between the manager and
    subordinates can increase the positiveness of
    the atmosphere of the firm.
    1. Morale can be improved.
    2. Productivity may be increased.
    3. Good communication requires a great
        deal of effort but it is worth the
        effort if a manager wants to
        successfully achieve the firm's
        goals.

QUESTIONS FOR REVIEW AND DISCUSSION

1. Why is human resource management important?

2. How is government influencing human resource management?

3. What methods do company's employ to develop managers?

4. Why is the performance review important to employee development?

5. Differentiate between direct and indirect compensation.

6. Discuss the various ways in which a person is separated from a company.

7. How does a company select personnel?

8. Why is it necessary for a manager to have good communication with subordinates?

9. What is communication?

10. What are the barriers to good communication?

11. What are the keys to good communication?

XIII
MANAGEMENT AND LABOR

I. What is a labor union?
    a) A labor union is when a group of workers join together to strive for common goals, e.g. employment security, better wages, improved benefits and better working conditions.

II. Differences between Craft Unions and Industrial Unions.
    a) A Craft Union is made up of skilled workers from the same trade, e.g. machinists and carpenters.
    b) An Industrial Union is made up of workers belonging to the same industry, e.g. auto unions and United Mineworkers.

III. Development of Unionism in The United States.
    a) Unionism began in the 1790's. Local groups of skilled workers in a particular craft joined to fight the division of labor and unfair hiring practices. To save money, employers divided skilled workers into teams to do only parts of jobs and hired women and children at extremely low wages to do other jobs. Most of the early unions disbanded after their demands were generally fulfilled.
    b) From the 1820s to the 1850s skilled workers such as carpenters and printers formed city-wide craft unions. Some local unions were able to form nationwide associations. However, because of the poor communication at this time, nationwide unions did not flourish. Because of poor economic conditions in the country, many unions went out of existence in the late 1830s, but were revived in the 1840s and 1850s as the economy improved. However, blacks and women were not allowed to join craft unions.
    c) The common law tradition carried to the U. S. from England held illegal the combining of men into a union, as well as the combining of businesses into a monopoly. In the early 19th century, most judges followed this line of reasoning. However, some of the unionists defied the courts and continued to strike, boycott, and demand (and sometimes obtain) collective bargaining rights. One

important advance came in 1842, when the Massachusetts State Supreme Court declared it legal for men to organize into a union and even to go out on strike for a closed shop.

d) Many American workers felt they should be organized because:
    1. Poor working conditions, unsanitary and unsafe.
    2. Low pay.
    3. Long hours.
    4. Lack of benefits.
    5. If injured on job there was no compensation and the employee was deemed to be at fault.
    6. Workers believed that there was strength in numbers.

e) Difficulties in organizing American labor:
    1. Problems of leadership.
    2. Public against it.
    3. Immigrants eager for work.
    4. Blacks working for low wages.
    5. Different groups in labor force were antagonistic to each other.
    6. Child labor.
    7. Women workers.
    8. Lockout.
    9. Blacklists.
    10. Culture of various areas of country (e.g. South) was strongly against unionism.
    11. Courts viewed with disfavor the growth of unionism.
    12. The traditional Protestants establishment viewed unionism as a product of immigrant groups.

f) During the first decades of the 19th century most of the small local unions were too weak to try militant action. Instead, they concentrated on mutual insurance schemes to provide members with sickness and death benefits. Moreover, many working class leaders felt that the only way to improve labor's position was through political action, not union organization. This group favored a public school system, free public land for the pioneer, and an end to the imprisonment of debtors. Education and the opportunity to acquire land would, they believed, make labor free.

g) Between 1820 and 1860, as the Industrial Revolution advanced, the number of factory workers almost quadrupled. The small local unions also grew larger, uniting in city associations and national craft unions. The Panic of 1837 and the eight year depression that followed caused the dissolution of many of these unions. However, with the return to prosperity, the organization of unions again progressed. Between five and ten national unions were in existence by the outbreak of the Civil War in 1861.

h) During the Civil War, there was a large demand for labor. This helped increase union membership. Many local unions and a minimum of ten additional national unions were founded. Among them was the first of the Big Four railroad unions, the Brotherhood of Locomotive Engineers (1863). But the Panic of 1873 and the following depression caused the union movement in The United States to become weaker.

i) Knights of Labor
    1. This union was founded in 1869 by Uriah S. Stephens.
    2. Its leader was Terrance V. Powderly.
    3. Organized on a national basis; with all workers invited to join its local lodges. Skilled and unskilled workers were invited to join.
    4. Demands of the Knights of Labor were considered to be extreme
        a. Abolition of Child Labor.
        b. Temperance.
        c. Equal pay for men and women.
        d. Establishment of cooperatively owned industrial plants.
        e. Eight-hour day.
        f. Taxes on incomes and inheritances.
        g. Workmen's compensation for industrial injuries.
        h. Postal savings banks.
        i. Government ownership of public utilities.
    5. The Knights of Labor failed due to factional fights within the organization

and a series of unsuccessful strikes.
The chief one was the Haymarket
Affair in 1886. Some maverick unions
went on strike for an eight-hour day.
They were joined by anarchists who
hoped thereby to spread their gospel
of violence. Soon Chicago was torn
by clashes between strikers, strike-
breakers and police. It was to pro-
test the shooting of four strikers by
police that the anarchists called a
rally in Haymarket Square on May 4,
1886. When police arrived, an un-
known person threw a bomb. The
explosion and the rioting which then
followed resulted in the death of
twelve people and the wounding of
many more.

6. Eight leading anarchists went on trial
for murder. The Haymarket Affair
was a very emotional issue at the
time. The Illinois Attorney demanded, "Convict these men, make examples of them, hang them, and you
save our institutions." The judge
distorted the law when he was
charging the jury. Influenced by
the mass hysteria of the time, the
jury condemned seven of the anarchists to death. Organized labor
rejected the anarchists but it was
too late in order to turn back the
roaring tide of public opinion which,
at that time, was strongly anti-labor
and anti-union. Eventually the anarchists sentenced to death were given
clemency by Governor Altgeld of
Illinois.

7. Shrinking to less than 100,000 members
by 1890, the Knights of Labor dis-
appeared in the late 1890's.

j) American Federation of Labor (A. F. of L)
a) One of the main reasons for the demise
of the Knights of Labor was its
failure to get strong support from
the established craft unions. A
number of these unions formed a
national organization of their own in
1881. Reorganized as the American

Federation of Labor in 1886, it put
its primary stress on realistic and
reasonable union objectives.
1. Only skilled workers--divided
into craft groups.
2. Samual Gompers was its
president from 1886-1924.
3. Eight-hour day.
4. Higher wages and better
working conditions.
a) The A. F. of L. grew slowly in its early
years. However, after 1898 membership climbed rapidly to a total of
e.g. 550,000 members in 1900. A
great upsurge in union membership
brought the total to 1,675,000 members in 1905, to 2,370,000 members
in 1917 and with World War I over,
there was another step forward to
over 4,000,000 in 1920. By 1920,
about 75% of all union workers
belonged to the A. F. of L.
k) Congress of Industrial Organiztions C.I.O.) -
1935
a) Formed in 1935 under the leadership
of John L. Lewis.
b) Unskilled and skilled workers could
belong to this union. This was
different from the A. F. of L.
where only skilled workers could
belong.
1) A. F. of L.-C.I.O. (1935)
a) The A. F. of L. and the C.I.O. were
rivals until 1955 when they joined
together in order to achieve gains
for labor.
b) George Meany became the leader of the
AFL-CIO.
c) Approximately one-half of the nearly 200
unions in The United States belong
to AFL-CIO.

IV. Key legislation in the American labor movement
a) Clayton Act (1914)
1. Called the Magna Carta of labor for it
specifically exempted unions from the
operation of the anti-trust laws.
2. Defined unfair methods of competition.

b) Adamson Act (1916)
　　1. Established an eight-hour day for railroad workers.
c) Railway Labor Act (1926)
　　1. Established legislation that provided for the peaceful settlement of disputes between the railroad companies and the railroad unions by the process of arbitration.
d) Norris-LaGuardia Act (1932)
　　1. Limited the use of court injunctions against union striking, picketing, boycotting.
　　2. Outlawed yellow-dog contracts which is when an employee agrees not to join a union while working for the company.
e) National Labor Relations Act (Wagner-Connery Act) – 1935
　　1. Gave legal recognition to labor unions.
　　2. Created National Labor Relations Board.
　　3. Protected workers against certain employer practices which hereafter would be considered illegal; such practices included discharging union organizers and interfering with the organizing of workers.
　　4. It held as legal secret elections of the workers in a plant, factory or store to determine which union was to be recognized as the collective bargaining agent for the workers.
　　5. Guaranteed labor the right to bargain collectively.
　　6. This act outlawed the company union.
f) Fair Labor Standards Act (1938)
　　1. Federal law which regulated women and children's work.
　　2. Regulated work performed at home.
　　3. Set minimum wages (at that time it was $0.25 per hour).
　　4. Made overtime rates compulsory.
g) Fair Employment Practices Committee (FEPC)
　　1. During World War II this committee was formed to protect workers from discrimination because of race, color,

or creed. A bill to make the FEPC
permanent was advocated by both
Republican and Democratic parties in
1944, but when such a measure was
introduced in Congress during 1945
it was talked to death by a filibuster
of southern congressmen.
  h) Taft-Hartley Act (1947)
    1. Reaffirmed right of worked to organize
       and bargain collectively.
    2. Prohibited unions from committing unfair
       labor practices such as
         a. refusing to bargain collec-
            tively with employers
         b. jurisdictional strikes
         c. featherbedding
         d. violating the term's of a
            union's contract
         e. secondary boycotts (sympa-
            thy strikes).
    3. Unions must file financial reports with
       the Secretary of Labor and union
       officials must sign statements that
       they are not members of the Com-
       munist party.
    4. Unions can't contribute to help the elec-
       tion campaigns of candidates for
       Federal office.
    5. Prohibited welfare funds contributed by
       the employer unless the employer
       has an equal voice with the union
       in the distribution of the funds.
    6. Provided for a 60-day cooling off period
       before a union could go out on
       strike. During this period, if a
       strike affects the national welfare,
       such as a railroad or a steel strike;
       the Federal government can secure
       a temporary injunction restricting
       the union from striking for addition-
       al days. During this time further
       efforts would be made to settle the
       dispute peacefully.
    7. Allowed right to work without joining a
       union (Section 44b).

i) The Landrum-Griffin Act (1959)
  1. Known as labor's Bill of Rights.
  2. Unions must file annual financial reports with the U. S. Department of Labor and such information must be made public.
  3. Union voting must be by secret ballot.
  4. Theft or embezzlement of union funds is a criminal offense.
  5. Union officers must be bonded.

V. Key Labor Terms
  a) Craft unions - consists of skilled workers in specific trades such as printers and carpenters.
  b) Industrial unions - consists of all workers in a particular industry such as the workers in the automobile industry or the textile industry, regardless of their occupation or skills.
  c) Jurisdictional strikes - resulting from disputes between two unions over who will represent a particular group of workers.
  d) Closed shop - is one in which every eligible worker in a shop must belong to the union. In addition the employer can only hire union members. This was forbidden by the Taft-Hartley Act.
  e) Wages are the hourly pay of an employee.
  f) Salary is the yearly pay of an employee.
  g) Certification occurs after the employees hold an election to determine if they want a specific union to represent them and with whom the employer must enter into collective bargaining. According to the Wagner-Connery Act, the National Labor Relations Board (NLRB) will not consider complaints brought by an uncertified union.
  h) Open shop - is a shop in which joining the union is voluntary.
  i) Union shop - an employer can hire any person he wishes but the new worker must join the union with a specific period of time.
  j) Agency shop - is one in which the employees do not have to join the union, but they must pay to the union a fee which is equal to union dues.
  k) Right-to-work laws - are state laws which forbid compulsory union membership.
  l) Featherbedding - workers get paid for work not done such as the fireman on the railroad.

m) <u>Secondary boycott</u> - work stoppage in order to force an employer to stop using the product of another company presently involved in a labor dispute.

VI. Management and Unions
    a) Management is usually against unions because of self-interest. They resent a reduction in their authority.
    b) Unionism makes the manager's job more difficult by increasing the amount of people whose approval must be received for a particular decision, and by presenting the risk that approval may not be received.
    c) Middle managers can be removed from their position but management cannot fire the union or its officials.
    d) Unionism increases the number of pressures that management must confront. The manager is caught between organized workers' demand for higher wages, customers for low prices and the stockholders and board of directors for larger profits.
    e) Most managers believe that unions, by limiting managerial initiative and discretion, hits directly at the roots of economic progress and rising national income. Therefore, they believe that unionism tends over the long-run to lessen rather than increase the real income of the working class.
    f) Most union leaders believe that they are assisting their members in achieving improvements in wages, benefits, and working conditions and are helping to achieve social progress.
    g) Managers and Union leaders also have differing outlooks because of their different personal background and experience. Two-thirds of top management officials in American corporations come from business and professional families. Three-quarters of top management have been to college Only a small percentage have engaged in manual labor at any stage in their careers.
    h) Day to day problems confronted by the factory workers are something that most managers have read about in college textbooks, but have not experienced first-hand.

i) In contrast is the background of the union offi-
cial, almost always a former worker, who is
short on formal training but has much experi-
ence as a factory worker. Thus, it is not
surprising that management and unions look
at industry differently and have differing
theories on personnel policy.
j) Unionism compels "management by policy" rather
than by impromptu decisions.

VII. Determining Labor-Management Disputes
   a) Collective bargaining - is a process of negotiation
      between management and union representa-
      tives for the purpose of arriving at mutually
      accepable pay, benefits and working condi-
      tions for the employees.
   b) Mediation - is the process of brining in an im-
      partial third party, called an arbitrator, into
      a union-management dispute. The mediator
      stands between the conflicting parties and
      makes recommendations which are not binding.
   c) Voluntary arbitration - is where both labor and
      management representatives decide to present
      the issues which are in dispute to an impar-
      tial third party.
   d) Compulsory arbitration - is when both labor and
      management representatives must submit their
      dispute to arbitration. The third party that
      usually requires this is the federal govern-
      ment.
   e) Grievance procedure - is a formal process which
      is part of the union contract that is used to
      settling differences between the union and
      management. Grievance handling starts when
      the aggrieved worker, or the union steward
      acting in behalf of the worker, or both the
      worker and the steward take the grievance
      to the employee's immediate superior. If the
      grievance cannot be resolved at this level,
      the dispute then goes up various levels in
      both the union and the firm. If the dispute
      is not settled at the various steps, it then
      goes to arbitration.

f)

Union Weapons	Management Weapons
1. Strikes – work stoppage by workers until the dispute is settled.	1. Lockout – manaagment shuts the firm in order to bring pressure upon the union to give in to management demands.
2. Picketing – workers parade at the entrance of the employer's place of business as a protest against management practice.	2. Injunction – is a court order which prohibits a particular labor practice.
3. Boycott – is an effort by the union to persuade people not to buy goods or services from a particular company.	3. Employer association – is a joint effort by employers to present a united front in order to deal more successfully with the labor unions.
4. Primary boycott – is one in which union members are instructed not to patronize the firm that is being boycotted.	

QUESTIONS FOR REVIEW AND DISCUSSION

1. Why were labor unions formed?

2. Why were there difficultires in organizing American labor?

3. Why did the American Federation of Labor succeed where-as the Knights of Labor failed?

4. Why did labor favor The National Labor Relations Act of 1935 while opposing The Taft-Hartley Act of 1947?

5. Explain:

    a) Craft Union

    b) Jurisdictional strikes

    c) Closed shop

    d) Union shop

    e) Agency shop

    f) Right-to-work laws

    g) Featherbedding

    h) Collective bargaining

    i) Yellow-dog contract

6. What are the main differences that confront management when dealing with unions? Can these differences be reconciled?

7. Describe the main weapons of unions in opposing management.

8. Describe the main weapons of management in opposing unions.

9. How powerful should unions become?

10. How powerful should management become?

11. What role should government play in settling labor-management disputes?

PART THREE

MARKETING

XIV

MARKETING

I. <u>Marketing</u> can be defined as the activities done by an
    organization with the purpose of influencing the
    customers of the organization's product and/or ser-
    vice.
    a) A company's production has to be marketed
        in order for the company to be success-
        ful.
    b) The 4 P's of marketing
        1. Product
        2. Place (distribution)
        3. Promotion
        4. Price.

II. The Marketing Concept
    a) The company must organize its activities to satis-
        fy its customers.
    b) The satisfaction of the customer's needs and de-
        sires is the central objective of the marketing
        function.

III. The Target Market
    a) The <u>target market</u> is the group of customers to
        whom the firm aims its marketing program -
        i.e., the young, the wealthy, males, females,
        sport fans, accountants, etc.
    b) Types of target markets
        1. <u>Industrial markets</u> - purchase goods to
            produce other goods and/or services
            - e.g. auto dealers purchase steel
            from a steel company in order to
            make an automobile.
            a. Industrial market has:
                1. smaller amount of
                    buyers
                2. buyers in general
                    are more knowl-
                    edgeable
                3. methods of buying
                    are more sys-
                    tematized.

2. <u>Consumer market</u> - purchase goods
and/or services for their own use -
i.e., a person buys an automobile
for himself to drive.
    a. Types of consumer goods
        1. convenience goods
        2. shopping goods
        3. specialty goods.
    b. How goods are typed is
dependent upon how the
consumer looks at it.

IV. Product Differentiation
    a) <u>Product differentiation</u> is a marketing strategy
which is used to convince consumers that a
particular product is different and better
than another product. Advertising is very
instrumental in emphasizing the distinctive-
ness of a product. An example of this is
the women's shampoo in which a lady says
that she pays more for the shampoo but she
is worth it.

V. <u>Market segmentation</u> is the act of dividing the market
into different parts so that one can direct their
marketing strategy towards particular groups. Market segmentation can be based on age, sex, ethnic
group, income group, geographical location, etc.
    a) Market segmentation attempts to develop a
special marketing mix for a particular
portion of the population.
    b) Market segmentation works under the assump-
tion that one product and/or service is
not sufficient to satisfy all buyers because of different tastes.

VI. <u>Marketing research</u> is the activity of using scientific
methodology to solve marketing problems.
    a) <u>Market research</u> is necessary for the pro-
ducer to learn what type of product the
public desires.
    b) Market research, if done correctly, can tell
the producer if there has been changes
in the desires of the public.

VII. Companies, in order to run more efficiently have to determine if the products that they are producing will
be well received by the public.
  a) Companies attempt to identify specific parts of
     the population to whom they can direct their
     marketing efforts.
     1. The population can be divided into vari-
        ous segments. These marketing seg-
        ments are based on:
        a. geographic
        b. age
        c. sex
        d. financial standing
        e. demographics
        f. educational background
        g. ethnic group
        h. religious group.
     2. Companies, in order to produce and
        market their product more efficiently,
        attempt to identify the reasons why
        the consumer purchases what he does.
        The more characteristics of the con-
        sumer that the firm can identify, the
        better will be the sales results.
        a. Therefore, marketers attempt to
           understand why the consumer
           purchases the way he does.
           This can be done by using:
           1. Sample surveys - is the
              polling of a statisti-
              cally representative
              portion of a partic-
              ular population.
           2. Decision model of pur-
              chases is the analy-
              sis of why a con-
              sumer buys what he
              does. There are
              five steps in the
              model:
              a. Recognizing a
                 need
              b. Gathering the
                 information
              c. Evaluating
                 various
                 alternatives

                                        d. Making the
                                            decision to
                                            purchase
                                        e. Evaluating the
                                            purchase.
        b) In order to maximize its efficiency, a busi-
            ness should have an idea of its potential
            sales of a product and/or service.   This
            can be done by:
                    1. Time series studies use past
                        sales information to predict
                        future sales.
                    2. Statistical analysis is a mathe-
                        matical model based on prob-
                        ability using various factors
                        to predict future sales
                        trends.
                    3. Test marketing is when a firm
                        chooses a sample group of
                        people usually a target mar-
                        ket, in order to see if the
                        product will not be accepted
                        by the target market.

QUESTIONS FOR REVIEW AND DISCUSSION

1. Explain the 4 P's of marketing.

2. How do industrial markets differ from consumer markets?

3. Why do marketers use product differentiation?

4. Why is market segmentation important to marketers?

5. Why are American marketers using more and more market-
        ing research?

6. Explain how a decision model works?

7. Which do you think is most effective; time series study,
        statistical analysis or test marketing? Why?

XV
MARKETING STRATEGY

I. As previously discussed, the marketing concept is a
    philosophy in which the needs of the consumer is
    given prime consideration.
    a) However, a profit can still be obtained. Find
        out what the consumer wants and pro-
        duce a product or service that will satis-
        fy that want. If the producer does this,
        a profit will be obtained.
        1. The marketing concept developed
            after World War II when the
            United States became a buy-
            er's market instead of a sell-
            er's market.

II. Functions of marketing:
    a) Marketing has more to it than the art of selling.
        Marketers are also needed to perform such
        functions as:
        1. Buying
        2. Transporting goods
        3. Storing goods
        4. Giving credit
        5. Taking financial risks
        6. Determining the quality of the goods
        7. Providing information
        8. Selling.

III. A market is one in which there are people who desire to
    buy the product or service, people who have the
    money to buy the item and people who have the au-
    thority to purchase the item. For example, a fifteen
    year old may want a Cadillac, has the money to pur-
    chase a Cadillac but can't buy the automobile because
    he or she is too young to enter into a contract to
    purchase.

IV. Consumer and industrial markets are divided in most
    cases. The seller usually uses the criterion of de-
    termining whether it is industrial or consumer by the
    purchaser's reason for buying the goods or service.
    a) If a purchaser buys the product or service
        to use it for himself, then the good or
        service is classified as a consumer good.
        If a person buys a house to serve as his
        domicile, he is buying a consumer good.

b) An industrial good is classified as such if the user's reason for buying the good or service is to use the good or service in the production of other goods or services that will eventually be resold.

V. Consumer behavior deals with all the aspects that cause people to buy goods and/or services. If consumers believe that what they need is important, they will be impelled to act. This need then becomes the motivation.
    a) Influences on consumer behavior
        1. What the consumer needs
        2. What the consumer desires
        3. The attitudes of the consumer
        4. The background of the consumer
        5. Family groups
        6. Social and cultural influences
        7. Political influences
        8. Economic influences
        9. Geographic groups
      10. Ethnic influences
      11. Religious influences
      12. Financial influences.

VI. Marketing research is the systematic gathering, recording, study and analysis of marketing information to help in making marketing decisions. The purpose of market research is to provide management with necessary information so that they can make more effective decisions.
    a) Marketing research information is compiled in the following ways:
        1. Internal data - these are records that one gets from the company itself - e.g. accounting records, personnel records, sales records, etc.
        2. External data - this is information one gets from sources outside the company - e.g. interviews with people, annual reports of other firms, etc.
        3. Primary data - this is original data that is the accumulation of one's own research. This data is accumulated by people from the company searching

through sales records, personnel records, territorial divisions, etc.

4. Secondary data is data that is not originally researched by the company. Secondary data is material which is provided by trade associations, government publications, books, articles, census figures from various departments of state, federal and local governments, etc. Secondary information is relied on by most companies rather than primary data because the cost of compiling it is less expensive.

QUESTIONS FOR REVIEW AND DISCUSSION

1. Explain the various functions of marketing.

2. How is a consumer good different from an industrial good?

3. Which are the three most important influences on consumer behavior? Why?

4. How is internal data different from external data?

5. How is primary data different from secondary data?

6. Why is market research important?

I. Product
  a) A product is any want-satisfying good, service
      or idea that possesses uses, values or bene-
      fits to the consumer. The product is ex-
      changed for money. You get paid for your
      good, service or idea.
  b) There are three classifications of consumer goods.
      1. Convenience goods are relatively inex-
          pensive goods that are bought with
          little efforts, such as soap, soda,
          milk, bread, cereal, etc.
      2. Shopping goods require some time and
          planning by the consumer. For ex-
          ample, a refrigerator, a television or
          a dishwasher are common shopping
          goods.
      3. Specialty goods are those goods in which
          the consumer spends much time doing
          research and evaluating alternatives.
          The consumer will make enormous
          efforts to satisfy his wants. Some
          examples of specialty goods are de-
          signer clothing, designer goods or a
          specific brand of medicine.

II. New Product Development has six steps
  a) Idea for a new product is conceived at this stage.
  b) Screening - is the stage that is used to separate
      the good ideas from the bad ideas.
  c) Analysis - is the analysis of a product or ser-
      vice to determine if it has growth potential
      and will ultimately pay for the company to
      produce it.
  d) Product Development - this is when the ideas for
      a new product are put into effect and a
      physical product is produced.
  e) Test Marketing - the product is tested to deter-
      mine consumer reaction so that management
      could make a decision whether to produce
      the goods for sale or not.
  f) Commercialization - this is the period when the
      firm decides to enter the market with full-
      scale production and marketing of the
      product.

III. Product Life Cycle

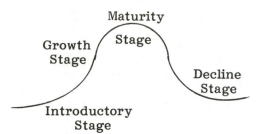

a) The introductory stage of the product life cycle
    usually has high costs, much modification,
    low sales, small profits and a high failure
    rates.
b) The growth stage of the product life cycle is
    usually characterized by the increase of
    sales and high profits.
c) The maturity stage of the product life cycle is
    when the growth of sales levels off. This
    stage usually has high promotion costs in
    order to maintain sales. Competition is also
    very strong - e.g. Coca-Cola and Pepsi-Cola.
d) The decline stage of the product life cycle is the
    period from when sales begin to decline until
    sales are stopped altogether. Profits are at
    their lowest.
e) Life cycles vary. Certain products will go
    through a life cycle in a few months while
    other products are still in their life cycle
    even though the product has been on the
    market for over one hundred years. A
    product should be carefully classified to meet
    the needs of the consumer. As a product
    evolves through the various stages of its
    life cycle, marketers have to make adjust-
    ments in the product in order to meet the
    changing desires of the consumer.

IV. Extension of a product's life cycle
    a) Many companies attempt to extend the life cycle
        of a product in a variety of ways. This is
        done because it is usually cheaper to keep
        an existing proven product in the market
        than taking the risk of developing a new
        product with its concommitant increase in
        uncertainty and expenses.

The marketing departments of various companies have used a variety of methods to try to extend the life of the products. Arm & Hammer, known for its baking soda, has found new uses for its product. These new uses for the product have brought new customers for Arm & Hammer. They have shown that Arm & Hammer baking soda can be used to eliminate odor in the refrigerator and can also be used for toothpaste. This increased use has added to the life cycle of the product. Sometimes, changes in the style and packaging of a product also extends the life cycle of the product. This is evident in many cereals and toothpastes.

1. A brand is a name or symbol which is used to identify a particular product so that the consumer can differentiate it from the competitors. Most people are familiar with Scotch Tape which is really cellophane tape, Kleenex which is really paper tissue, Pampers which is really disposable diapers and Xerox which is really photographic copying.

2. Many consumers prefer to buy products that are familiar brands to them because:
   a. They have confidence in something they know
   b. They have faith in the quality of the product
   c. Familiarity may breed a certain amount of assurance
   d. They feel loyalty to a particular brand - "I will only buy a Buick."

QUESTIONS FOR REVIEW AND DISCUSSION

1. Explain the steps in the development of a new product.

2. Explain the various stages in the product life cycle.

3. Why do many companies try to extend the life cycle of a product rather than abandoning the production of that product?

XVII
PRODUCTION

I. <u>Production</u> is the use of people and machinery to change unfinished materials into finished products or services.

    a) <u>Peter F. Drucker</u> - "Production is not the application of tools to materials. It is the application of logic to work."

II. The United States has become the leading industrial nation in the world. One reason has been the abundance of resources which we possess. Another reason has been our capitalistic (free and private enterprise) economic system. Because of our free enterprise system, mass production has been able to flourish.

    a) <u>Mass production</u> is the production of goods in large quantities, usually be the use of machinery. Certain factors such as specialization, mechanization and standardization are involved in mass production.

        1. <u>Specialization</u> is the breaking down of work into its simplest parts, therefore allowing the worker to become proficient in one aspect of the production process.

        2. <u>Mechanization</u> is the use of machinery to replace human labor.

        3. <u>Standardization</u> is the producing of uniform and interchangeable parts. The process of standardization was developed by Eli Whitney, the discoverer of the cotton gin.

III. <u>Inputs</u> are the resources that go into the making of a product or service.

    a) <u>Raw materials</u> such as iron, yarn, unfinished meta, etc.

    b) <u>Capital goods</u> such as machinery and factory buildings.

    c) <u>Human resources</u> such as skilled labor, etc.

IV. Types of production systems:
    a) <u>Intermittent process</u> is a process that stops and starts depending upon the product made - i.e., heavy equipment producers.
        1. <u>Job-order</u> production is an intermittent process that occurs at the request of a specific order to fill a customer's needs.
        2. <u>Lot-order</u> is an intermittent process used to fill inventory needs.
    b) <u>Continuous flow</u> produces a standardized item which is carried in inventory. For example, certain items in the textile industry are standardized items and therefore some textile mills keep the looms running 168 hours a week putting out these standardized goods.
    c) Kind of investment
        1. <u>Capital-intensive</u> is when a great deal of money is invested in machinery so that a relatively small amount of labor is employed - i.e. automated production.
        2. <u>Labor-intensive</u> is when a great deal of labor is used - i.e. making of individually made key chains.
    d) <u>Analytic system of production</u> is the method by which a raw material is broken down into its component parts in order to extract products from it - i.e. oil can be extracted from some farm products.
    e) <u>Synthetic system of production</u> is the process of combining various raw materials into a finished product - i.e. an automobile from iron.

V. Production Management
    a) <u>Production management</u> is the applying of managerial principles to the production function.
        1. The major parts of the production function are:
            a. Planning for production
            b. Installing the facility for production
            c. Controlling and organizing the production process.

VI. Planning Production
    a) Decide the product or service to be produced.
    b) Certain questions must be answered.
        1. What should be produced?
        2. Why should it be produced?
        3. How much of it can be produced?
        4. What style and features should the product have?
        5. Can it be produced for a profit?
        6. Should we "make or buy" some of the items needed in the production process?
            a. One has to determine whether to produce some of the components themselves or obtain them from a supplier.

VII. Location of the Plant
    a) The location of the plant is determined by a number of factors such as:
        1. Proximity to markets
        2. Proximity to raw materials
        3. Proximity to qualified personnel
        4. Proximity to energy needs
        5. Proximity to transportation
        6. Living conditions in the local community so as to be able to attract skilled people - i.e. schools, hospitals, etc.
        7. Favorable political climate. The local community desires to have the plant.
        8. Other - lower taxes, tax abatements, local area provides training programs, etc.

VIII. Layout of Production Facilities
    a) Product layout is a set-up where only a few products are produced but in great quantities.
    b) Process layout is a set-up that produces a variety of products in small amounts.
    c) Fixed-production layout locates the product in a permanent position. Employees and materials are brought to and from it.
    d) Customer-oriented layout is a layout which is set up for easier relations between the customer and the firm.

IX. Staffing for Production
  a) <u>Staffing for production</u> deals with obtaining the best application of personnel to the production process.
  b) Problem of hiring qualified staff:
    1. Are there enough qualified people available?
    2. Can we train the necessary people?
    3. Can we retrain them when necessary?
    4. What are the local, state and federal restrictions?
    5. Are there union restrictions or other problems - i.e. seniority, etc.

X. Production Control
  a) <u>Controlling</u> is the act of setting a certain degree of standards and checking the different types of production at different times and making the necessary corrections when appropriate.
  b) The Gantt Chart
        This is a production-control device. In this chart, the available amount of time for each part of the production process is broken down by hours. Each job is then determined for each division. The Gantt chart also shows how much time it actually took to do the job. In this way, the person in charge of scheduling in the production process can observe if the planning is sufficient and can make corrections when necessary.

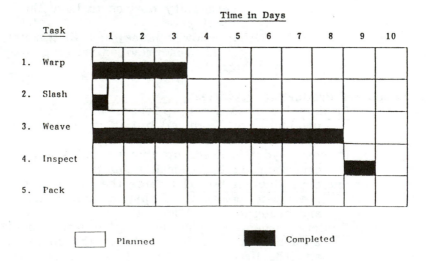

116

c) PERT (Project Evaluation and Review Technique)
  1. PERT is a method of scheduling that uses network diagrams to facilitate and coordinate complex methods of production.
  2. The PERT chart helps the manager organize what should be produced when and how long it is necessary to complete each process.
      a. The manager lists each step in the process and how long it would take to complete each step.
      b. The manager then arranges the steps in the order necessary for completion.
      c. The manager then draws a diagram showing how each step is related to the other.
      d. One set of steps is the critical path. A critical path in a PERT chart is a series of operations that takes the greatest length of time to complete, provided there isn't any waste of time.
          1. The operations in the critical path are the ones in which time limits are the most important.
          2. A delay in any operation in the critical path delays the entire production process.
  3. PERT charts are used on such jobs as the building of large office and/or residential buildings.

4. PERT charts, at times, have thousands of steps covering many months (and at times, years) of production. Presently, computers are replacing individuals in developing complex PERT charts.

d) Routing is the aspect of production control that sets the work sequence in the plant.

e) Scheduling is the aspect of production control that sets timetables of how long each activity takes.

f) Materials requirement planning (MRP) is a computer based planning program that makes sure that materials needed for production are available in the right amount and at the right location.

g) Dispatching tells each division what job is to be done and how much time is allotted for the job to be completed.

h) Follow-up notices problems during the production process and tells management what corrections should be done.

i) Maintenance is important in the control of plant and equipment.

1. Preventive maintenance can save a great deal of money for a company by reducing the amount of downtime.

j) Inventory control is the keeping of enough supplies to enable production to continue at a steady pace while attempting to keep the costs of carrying inventory as low as possible.

1. The level of inventory tries to balance the costs of maintaining a high inventory level against the chance and the concurrent problems that one faces if one runs out of stock.

2. High Inventory versus Low Inventory

High Inventory	Low Inventory
a. Investment in material instead of putting the money into CD's, Treasury bills, etc.	a. Risk of running out of goods.
b. Storage costs.	b. Customers might be dissatisfied and this can cost the firm sales.
c. Certain kinds of goods might spoil or deteriorate.	

XI. Materials Management

    a) The purchasing of goods and materials is vital to earning a profit in a business. Careful purchasing can save a company a great deal of money.

        1. Sources of the necessary goods and/or services needed for production must be able to provide enough volume, quality and on-time delivery.

    b) The purchasing process should take advantage of buying in volume, demanding acceptable quality because of buying in volume, and having specialized knowledge of the purchasing product.

    c) Purchasing practices should:

        1. Buy when the price is right

        2. Either have a policy of buying from few sources where one gets certain advantages or using as many sources of supply as possible so if one supplier starts raising the prices or goes out of business, the company is not stuck without a supplier.

        3. Bill of materials is a listing of all materials needed to produce a product and/or service.

d) Many companies use the following when purchasing:
1. Value analysis - this involves re-
viewing specifications of various
materials in order to identify un-
necessary costs.
2. Vendor analysis - evaluates various
suppliers in terms of price and
quality.
3. Competitive bidding encourages different suppliers to bid against
one another in order to get a
more favorable price.

V. Quality Control
a) Quality control of products and/or services are
measured against established quality standards of the particular industry involved.
b) Quality circles are groups of employees (usually
not more than fifteen in number) from the
same division who get together to analyze
and solve problems in the work place.
c) Pollution is unwanted air, noise, water and material excretions from production.
1. Costs incurred in controlling pollution should be figured in the
total cost of production.

QUESTIONS FOR REVIEW AND DISCUSSION

1. Define production.

2. Differentiate between specialization, mechanization and standardization.

3. Explain the major parts of the production function.

4. What questions should be answered in planning production?

5. Which factors are the most important in determining the location of a production facility?

6. How does the Gantt Chart and PERT contribute to production control?

7. Discuss the problems involved in having high or low inventory.

8. Why is quality control becoming of greater importance to American producers?

XVIII
PRICE DETERMINATION

I. Price is very important in a capitalist economy. This is
    because price provides the means by which the value
    of goods or services can be expressed in a way that
    everyone understands, money.
    a) Without prices, the amount of goods pro-
        duced and the rate in which they move
        through the various channels of distrib-
        ution could not be achieved. People are
        in business to make a profit. There-
        fore, people in the channels or distrib-
        ution have to set a price (value) on
        their goods and services. If they do
        not achieve what they believe to be a
        fair value for their goods and services,
        they will not sell their goods or perform
        their services.

II. The price of a product is generally related to the cost
     of producing that particular product.
     a) Cost-oriented approach to pricing is when a
         company depends chiefly on the cost of
         production as the basis for setting the
         price of its product.
     b) Fixed costs are those costs that cannot be
         changed in the short-run such as mort-
         gage, rent and taxes.
     c) Variable costs are those costs that can be
         changed in the short-run, such as labor
         (paying for voertime), material and
         energy.
     d) Total costs are the total of fixed costs plus
         variable costs.

III. When an item is usually put up for sale, a price is in
      most cases determined for it. The seller usually
      does not ask the purchaser what price he is willing
      to pay for the item. Exceptions are auction sales
      where people bid for the item and casual sales where
      a neighbor will sell his automobile to another person.

IV. Markup factors that contribute to the determination of prices:

    a) Markup percentage

          1. Retail price markup

Retail price	$ 10	(100%)
Cost	5	
Markup	$ 5	(50% of the retail price)

          2. Cost markup method

Cost	$5	(100%
Markup	$3	(60% of cost)
Retail price	$8	

V. Price Policies

    a) Price lines are a group of pre-set prices that are the only ones at which the items are sold. For example, items in some areas may be offered for sale at $1.99, $2.99 or $3.99.

    b) Price leadership is when in certain industries, there are leaders who set their prices without worrying about what other companies in the industry are charging. For example, Milliken & Co. in textiles is a price leader due to its size and prestige.

    c) Suggested prices is when the producer puts a suggested retail price on his product. Retailers are free to charge that price or to charge a lesser price in order to show the consumer that he is receiving a good deal when he is purchasing the product.

    d) What the traffic will bear is a very common price policy. Many people who are in their respective business for a long time know just how much they can sell their product for. They are fully aware of what their customers are willing to spend for the product. Therefore, they are familiar with the upper price limits they can charge their customers without their customers abandoning them for other producers.

    e) Elastic demand occurs when the price of an item is changed because there is a great change in the demand for the item. For example, when automobile dealers give weekend specials in which there is a great decrease in the price of the cars, there is usually a large increase in sales. This shows demand elasticity.

f) Inelasticity of demand is the opposite of elastic demand. An example of inelasticity of demand is salt. Regardless of the price for salt, people will use only a certain amount and no more.

g) Monopoly price is when one company controls the price. In certain industries this occurs. For example, in the utilities industry this occurs. Though there is public relations of the utilities, in reality they are still a monopoly.

h) Monopolistic competition is when many competitors control a certain portion of the market due to some distinctive aspect of their product. For example, one may purchase a certain brand of toothpaste with a particular fluoride formula. The company that puts out this brand controls the formula and is the only one selling this type. However, if they refused to sell the toothpaste, the consumer can still go out and purchase toothpaste. The company controls a portion of the market, not all of the market.

QUESTIONS FOR REVIEW AND DISCUSSION

1. Why is price important in a capitalist economy?

2. How is the price of a product related to the cost of producing a particular product?

3. How is a retail price markup different from the cost markup method?

4. How is monopoly price different from monopolistic competition?

5. How is elastic demand different from inelasticity of demand?

6. Do you believe that the government should regulate prices? Why?

XIX

DISTRIBUTION

I. <u>Channels of distribution</u> are the different routes that
    goods travel when moving from the producer to the
    ultimate consumer.
    a) <u>Intermediaries</u> are people or companies in the
       channel of distribution that operate be-
       tween the producer of the goods and the
       ultimate consumer purchaser or the ulti-
       mate industrial purchaser.
       1. <u>Marketing intermediaries</u> are
          those who are in the channel
          of distribution between the
          producer and the ultimate
          purchaser.
       2. <u>Wholesaling (Jobber) intermedi-
          aries</u> are those who sell
          chiefly to retailers or to
          other wholesalers or indus-
          trial purchasers.
    b) Channels of distribution for consumer goods.
       1. Producer ⟶ consumer
       2. Producer ⟶ retailer ⟶ consumer
       3. Producer ⟶ wholesaler ⟶ retailer
          ⟶ consumer
       4. Producer ⟶ broker or agent ⟶
          wholesaler ⟶ retailer ⟶
          consumer
    c) Channels of distribution for industrial goods
       1. Producer ⟶ industrial user
       2. Producer ⟶ wholesaler ⟶ indus-
          trial user
       3. Producer ⟶ agent or broker ⟶
          wholesaler ⟶ industrial user
    d) Marketing channels are made up of two
       basic marketing institutions, wholesaling
       and retailing.

II. <u>Wholesalers</u> are those intermediaries who purchase prod-
    ucts from the producer and sell them to other
    wholesalers, retailers, industrial users and many
    local, state and federal government agencies.
    a) <u>Wholesaling functions:</u>
       1. Perform storage, financing, risk-
          taking, market information and
          assembling of goods

2. Break large orders received from suppliers into smaller shipments for the retailer, thereby saving the retailer money
3. Represent, as a sales force, a number of manufacturers, thereby reducing costs
4. Represent, as purchasers, a number of retailers, thereby reducing costs
5. There are three categories of wholesalers:
   a. Manufacturer owned wholesaler
   b. Retailer owned wholesaler
   c. Independent wholesaler.

III. <u>Retailers</u> are marketing intermediaries or meddlemen who obtain goods from either wholesalers, brokers and agents, and sell them to the ultimate consumer.
   a) The great majority of retail stores are owner-manager.
      1. This is because retailing is a relatively easy business to get into because:
         a. There are small financial requirements
         b. There are few legal requirements
         c. There are no formal educational requirements.
      2. The rate of failure in small retail stores is very high (over 50%) because competition is very stiff. In addition, because of the ease of entering the retail business, many unqualified people start a retail business without having the tools to make it a success.
      3. Many people are familiar with large retailers such as Macy's, Sears, Safeway, K-Mart and J. C. Penney.

b) Since <u>retailing</u> deals with all the activities concerned with the sale of goods and services to the ultimate consumer, one will find a variety of retail establishments.

1. Types of retail stores:
   a. <u>Department stores</u> – carry a wide variety of goods grouped into different departments - e.g. Macy's.
   b. <u>Specialty stores</u> sell only one kind of product such as children's shoes of men's clothing.
   c. <u>Discount stores</u> emphasize high volume and low prices. They sell goods at low prices because they get a great number of goods at liquidation sales.
   d. <u>Factory outlets</u> is a type of retailing operation where the manufacturer sells the consumer.
   e. <u>Catalog stores</u> show items for display and bring the goods from a different location to the pick-up area - e.g. Sears catalog.
   f. <u>Supermarkets</u> are large self-service food stores who also sell non-fiid items. Such stores are A & P, Shop-Rite, Grand Union, Pathmark, Foodtown, etc.
   g. <u>Variety stores</u> offer the consumer many kinds of small, inexpensive goods.

Examples of these
type of stores are
Woolworth and Ben
Franklin.

h. Hypermarkets are large
establishments that
sell food and non-
food items. In addi-
tion, they have sepa-
rate stores attached
to the market such
as liquor stores,
gourmet shops,
photography stores,
etc. Many malls are
built around this
type of store.

i. Warehouse stores are
similar to super-
markets but the con-
sumer receives little
assistance. By cut-
ting the cost of
labor, these stores
attempt to reduce
the price to the con-
sumer.

j. Convenience stores sell
food and non-food
items. They are
open on holidays and
during off-hours.
They usually charge
high prices in ex-
change for the con-
venient hours.
Examples of conven-
ience stores are
"Convenient Stores"
and "Seven-Eleven."

c) Non store (direct) retailing has grown dra-
matically in recent years. These direct
retailers sell directly to the consumer
via television, door-to-door sales, vend-
ing machiens and mail order.

d) The wheel of retailing is the terminology
used to describe the constant state of
change that retailing is in.

1. New retailers are constantly
entering the market as low
cost, low price, low service
operations.
2. Eventually the low service
retailer upgrades his store,
moves to a fancier location
where he sells better quality
goods at higher prices.
Therefore, he creates a void
in the lower portions of the
retail market for a new low
cost, low price, low service
enterprise to fill.

IV. Physical distribution includes transportation of goods,
the handling of materials, the processing of orders
and the control of merchandise (inventory).
a) Transportation is the moving of goods from
one place to another. This includes
truck, railroad, airplane, ship and pipeline.
b) Handling of materials involves the receiving,
storing, sorting and sending the proper
goods out at the proper time.
c) Order processing deals with the filling of a
customer's orders as quickly and efficiently as possible.
d) Inventory control is a method of seeing that
enough merchandise is available to meet
customer needs while attempting to keep
the costs of inventory as low as possible.

QUESTIONS FOR REVIEW AND DISCUSSION

1. Describe the various channels of distribution.

2. Why are the channels of distribution for many consumer goods so long?

3. Why are the channels of distribution shorter for the industrial user than for the consumer?

4. Explain the functions that the wholesaler performs.

5. Why is it relatively easy to enter the field of retailing?

6. Do shopping centers and malls offer the retailer any advantages? Why?

7. Which type of retail stores are growing the fastest? Why?

8. Explain what is meant by the wheel of retailing.

9. Which is the most important aspect in the physical distribution of goods?

XX

PROMOTION

I. <u>Promotion</u> is a company's total effort to make the public
aware of its product. Promotion is the communica-
tive aspect of marketing. Its objective is to be
persuasive in order to enlarge the use of a particular product and/or service. In order to enlarge the
use of its product or service, promoters will try to
gain attention for its product or service. Part of
promotion's function is to inform, persuade and re-
mind the consumers for the purpose of increasing
sales or maintaining a positive attitude from its pre-
present customers.

    a) There are four tools in the <u>promotional mix</u>.

        1. <u>Advertising</u> is any paid promotion
of items towards a group of peo-
ple, whether a small or a large
group. Advertising media is
television, radio, newspapers,
magazines and direct mail.

        2. <u>Publicity</u> is any advertising that a
company receives from the media
without paying the media; i.e.,
press releases. Many firms
maintain public relations departments in order to improve the
firm's image with the public.

        3. <u>Sales promotion</u> is any effort to
promote sales by ways other
than advertising or personal
selling - e.g. free samples,
coupons, contests, etc.

        4. <u>Personal selling</u> is the act of a
salesperson personally selling
the product to a customer. This
can be done on the retail level
or with a salesperson calling on
a customer in the field.

    b) <u>Promotional strategy</u> is determined by a
variety of factors.

        1. Type of product
        2. Size of the budget
        3. Stage in the product life cycle
        4. Target market
        5. Marketing philosophy of the
firm.

II. Advertising
    a) An advertising agency serves its customers (the call their customers "clients") by:
        1. Planning advertising campaigns
        2. Choosing the media - e.g. radio, T.V., newspapers, magazines, etc.
    b) The A.I.D.A. process
        1. Attention
        2. Interest
        3. Desire
        4. Action.
    c) Kinds of Advertising
        1. Selective or brand advertising tries to persuade people to buy a particular brand.
            a. Dewar's Scotch tries to appeal to upscale people.
            b. "Miller Time" attempts to appeal to the blue collar group.
            c. Budweiser tries to appeal to various groups by "this Buds for you."
        2. Primary demand advertising attempts to increase demand for a product as a whole and not a specific brand. For example, due to the widespread belief that too much meat increases your cholesterol content, the meat dealers have been advertising to the public that people should purchase meat because meat is healthy for them. They do not push any specific brand but meat as a whole.
    d) Objectives of advertising are to:
        1. Inform and thereby increase demand for a product - e.g. condoms.
        2. Persuade in order to affect a specific market's attitudes or behavior - e.g. Miller Lite with Rodney Dangerfield.
        3. Reinforce in order to keep the customers you have - e.g. Coca-Cola and Pepsi-Cola.
    e) Institutional advertising tries to increase the image of the people doing the advertising - e.g. Mormons.

f) Advertising takes place in the following:
1. Radio
2. Television
3. Newspapers
4. Magazines
5. Billboards
6. Direct mail
7. Shopping guides
8. Point-of-purchase displays.

III. Publicity
a) Publicity is the attempt to communicate, through the various media, information that can be interpreted as legitimate news stories. Of course, it is hoped that the publicity would be favorable.
1. Public relations deals with any communication with the general public or with businesses or government that attempts to foster goodwill and a favorable image for the company.
a. Businesses issue press releases telling about the good things that the firm is doing.

IV. Sales Promotion
a) Sales promotion tries to create special situations that will call attention to the firm and increase sales.
b) There are many types of sales promotions such as:
1. Contests
2. Games
3. Sweepstakes
4. Coupons
5. Point-of-purchase displays
6. Trading stamps
7. Sponsorship of entertainment events
8. Sponsorship of athletic events
9. Sponsorship of various charities
10. Samples
11. Demonstrations.
c) The promotional blend is affected by the nature of the product, the market one is competing in and the amount of money available for promotion.

V. Personal Selling
    a) Personal selling is a part of a company's overall marketing objectives. Selling objectives differ from firm to firm depending in great part on the company's product or service and the customers they have and the potential customers they wish to attract.

    b) The job of the sales person consists of:
1. Searching out prospective customers
2. Discovering what the customer wants and needs
3. Fill the need of the customer
4. Gives sales presentations
5. Closes the sale
6. Follow-up to satisfy customer and get new sales leads.

    c) The system of compensation for the sales forces is very important in obtaining productivity from the sales people.
1. Methods of compensation of the sales force:
    a. Salary
    b. Commission
    c. Salary + commission
    d. Salary + bonus
    e. Commission + bonus.

QUESTIONS FOR REVIEW AND DISCUSSION

1. Why do company's promote their products or services?

2. Describe the promotional mix.

3. Which is the most important objective of advertising? Why?

4. Why are certain industries resorting to primary demand advertising?

5. Why do many companies have public relations departments?

6. Which type of sales promotion do you favor the most?

7. Which system of compensation is best for a professional sales force? Why?

XXI

MANAGEMENT INFORMATION SYSTEMS

I.   Information is vital for any manager to form intelligent
     decisions about a firm's competition, consumers,
     production, scheduling, shipping, payroll, etc.
     Computers are becoming more and more important in
     the development of management information systems.
     a)   A management information system (MIS) is a
          systematic method of enabling manage-
          ment to have past, present and predi-
          cated future information about the com-
          pany's internal and external situations.
          The more information a firm has, the
          greater its chances for a successful
          operation of its business.

II. Information may be obtained from many sources.
     a)   Internal data is information acquired from the
          company's own records. The information
          comes from:
                    1.   Income statements
                    2.   Balance sheets
                    3.   Production records
                    4.   Purchase records
                    5.   Shipping records
                    6.   Personnel records.
     b)   External data is information acquired from vari-
          ous sources outside the company:
                    1.   Government sources – information
                         given by the Department of
                         Commerce, Federal Reserve
                         System, Department of Labor
                         and the Department of Housing
                         and Urban Development among
                         the great many government
                         sources.
                    2.   Private sources – various publica-
                         tions such as the Wall Street
                         Journal, Business Week, indus-
                         trial and trade magazines, etc.
                    3.   Competitors – various types of infor-
                         mation about competitors can be
                         obtained from public and private
                         sources.

III. Primary and Secondary Data
      b) <u>Primary data</u> is original research or data which is assembled for the first time. This is usually done by survey, observation and experimentation. For example, many soft-drink companies ask people to taste a type of drink with or without a specific ingredient in order to see if the public likes the drink or not.
      c) <u>Secondary data</u> is material that has been gathered by others. For example, firms obtain information from newspapers, magazines, journals, government sources, etc. Firms will most likely use secondary data whenever they can because it is much less expensive to obtain than primary data.

IV. <u>Statistics</u> is an area of mathematics that deals with the collection, analysis and presentation of numerical information.
      a) A <u>statistic</u> is a fact expressed in numerical form.
      b) The three kinds of statistics that are used to show central tendency are mean, median and mode.
          1. <u>Mean</u> is the average number in a series of numbers.

$$
\begin{array}{c}
4 \\
6 \\
10 \\
12 \\
3 \\
\hline
5\,\overline{\smash)35} = 7 \longleftarrow \text{mean}
\end{array}
$$

          2. <u>Median</u> is the middle number when there are the same amount of numbers above and below the number in a series of numbers.

$$
\begin{array}{l}
2 \\
3 \\
4 \\
5 \longleftarrow 5 \text{ is the median} \\
6 \qquad\quad\ \text{number} \\
7 \\
8
\end{array}
$$

3. <u>Mode</u> is the number that appears most often in a series of numbers.

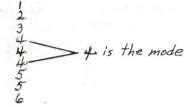

V. Presentation of Data

a) <u>Bar graph</u> – is used when statistics are compared.

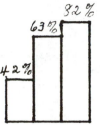

b) <u>Pie chart</u> – is a graphic method in which a pie is divided proportionally.

c) <u>Line chart</u> is a method which is used in order to demonstrate trends.

QUESTIONS FOR REVIEW AND DISCUSSION

1. Why does a business need a management information system?

2. How is mean, median and mode different?

3. How is primary data different from secondary data?

4. How is internal data different from external data?

XXII
QUANTITATIVE DECISION MAKING

I. The Computer
    a) A computer is a machine that can store, process and recall data with speed, accuracy and memory.
    b) Computer processing is a flow pattern in which data is collected, transformed into machine readable form and is used as the input. The computer then peocesses the input by using mathematical calculations which results in the output.

$$\boxed{Input} \rightarrow \boxed{Processing} \rightarrow \boxed{Output}$$

    c) Data processing is the technique of collecting and using data, e.g. Electronic Data Processing (EDP).
    d) Data are numbers, facts, letters, etc.

II. Historical Overview
    a) Blaise Pascal, in 1642 developed an adding machine.
            1. Gottfried Leibnitz then built a machine that could add, subtract, multiply and figure square roots.
            2. Charles Babbage, in the 1820s built a mathematical machine that could do a variety of complex calculations without the help of humans.
    b) Herman Hollerith, during the 1880's built a machine with the ability to code date for the United States Bureau of the Census. By using a system of punched cards with census information on them, 250 cards were able to be sorted within sixty seconds.
            1. The Mark I was developed about 1940. This was the first automatic calculator. It was able to multiply ten digit numbers within a three second time period.
            2. The ENIAC (Electronic Numerical Integrator and Calculator) was introduced around 1945 and was able to compute 300 numbers within a cone second time period.

3. In 1951, the United States Bureau
of the Census used the Sperry
Rand computed called the
UNIVAC I.
a. Gradually computer
technology grew from
vacuum tube memory
to the use of tran-
sistors to the present
time of using solid
state technology.

III. Within the last few decades computers have become a
more and more vital aspect of business organization.
a) Hardware is the physical components of the
computer.
b) Software are the instructions which tell the
computer what to do.

IV. Advantages of using computers for the processing of
business data are:
a) Large amounts of company records can be
maintained at a relatively low cost
b) Speed in processing and retrieval of records
c) Reduction in labor costs
d) Increased accuracy
e) Data storage is more efficient.

V. Components of the computer are:
a) Input devices of the computer serve the function
of routing data from a source to the Central
Processing Unit (CPU) of the computer.
b) Central Processing Unit (CPU) - is known as the
"brains of the computer." It is in the CPU
that the actual processing of data occurs.
The CPU has three chief components.
1. Storage - memory part of the
computer where data is stored.
2. Control unit - informs the computer
of what it should do and where
to put the information.
3. Arithmetic unit - performs mathematical computations.
c) Output devices - are the end-product. They
permit the computer to report its information.

VI.   Computer Programs
a)   A <u>complete program</u> is the set of instructions telling the computer what calculations it should perform.
1.   BASIC is a simplified language for programming a computer (Beginner's All-Purpose Symbolic Instruction Code).
2.   COBAL is the standard business language for programming a computer (Common Business Orienter Language).
3.   FORTRAN (Formula Translation) – used for the sciences.
4.   PL/I (Programming Language) – this computer language is used for both business and science.

VII.   Computers help managers in making decisions:
a)   Scheduling of production
b)   CAD – Computer-Aid-Design – using computer graphics to aid in analyzing and designing
c)   Keeping of records
d)   Billing of customers
e)   Personnel information
f)   Preparing the company payroll
g)   CAM – Computer Aided Manufacturing – using machines that are computer controlled in the manufacturing process.

VIII.   Computers are presently being used in such businesses as textiles, railroads, airlines, banks, stock market, various kinds of engineering, medicine, law enforcement, etc.
Whether or not a firm decides to install a computer system, it has to determine if it is feasible to convert to a computer system. The firm should determine: Will the computer system be cost effective? Can the computer system be used efficiently? Will the employees accept the new system?

QUESTIONS FOR REVIEW AND DISCUSSION

1. Do computers create unemployment? Why?

2. How do computers help managers in making decisions?

3. Describe the components of the computer.

4. Discuss the pros and cons of using a computer in business.

5. Describe the functions of the main computer programs.

PART FOUR

FINANCE

I. What is accounting?
    a) Accounting is the recording, classifying, inter-
        preting and transmitting the financial activi-
        ties of a business firm.
        1. Private accountants are those who
            work for companies or the local,
            state or federal government.
        2. Public accountants perform such
            accounting duties as auditing
            and certifying financial state-
            ments.
        3. Managerial accounting provides
            information to various managers
            within the firm to enable them
            to make better decisions.
        4. Financial accounting provides infor-
            mation to people outside the firm
            such as the public, creditors
            and government.
    b) A bookkeeper is different from an accountant.
        The bookkeeper records the day-to-day
        business activities. This is mainly a me-
        chanical job and a bookkeeper is considered
        a clerical job. An accountant is considered
        a professional who analyzes and interprets
        financial data.
    c) Accounting documents:
        1. Payroll records
        2. Sales records
        3. Shipping records
        4. Travel records
        5. Entertainment records
        6. Bank statements
        7. Purchasing records
        8. Miscellaneous records - e.g. petty cash,
            others, etc.
    d) The five main accounts in the accounting pro-
        cess are assets, liabilities, owners' equity,
        revenue and expenses.
        1. Assets is anything of value that a
            company owns.
            a. Current assets are cash
                or anything that can
                be converted into cash
                within a year.

b. Accounts receivable are
what is owed to a com-
pany by its customers.
c. Inventory is the stock
that a firm has for sale.
d. Fixed assets is anything
of value owned by the
busines but is not for
sale, i.e., buildings,
equipment, land.
e. Intangible assets is a non-
physical asset, extreme-
ly difficult to measure,
but is very important
to a company's stature
in the marketplace.
Examples of intangible
assets are a company's
good will and reputation.
2. Liabilities are what the firm owes to
others. Liabilities are debts.
They are the sum of money the
company owes to other firms or
individuals.
a. Current liabilities are
debts that the firm has
to repay in a year or
less.
b. Long term liabilities or
fixed liabilities are
debts that the firm
must repay over a
period greater than
one year.
c. A few examples of liabilities are:
1. Accounts payable
which is money
owed for mer-
chandise
bought on
credit.
2. Amounts of money
owed on bonds.
3. Expenses which
the company
has not yet
paid.

3. <u>Owners' equity</u> is the owner's worth or value. They include such items as securities, cash, buildings, automobiles, etc. Owners' equity is the portion of a company's assets that belong to the owners after all obligations to all others creditors have been filled.

   a. The accounting formula which shows owners' equity is:

$$A - L = OE$$

Assets minus liabilities = Owners' Equity

     1. This accounting formula $A - L = OE$ can be interpreted in the following manner.

What you <u>OWN</u> <u>minus</u> what you <u>OWE</u> = Owners' <u>Equity</u>

     2. Assets minus <u>Liabilities</u> = <u>Owners' Equity</u> is the key for the financial statement known as the <u>balance sheet</u>.

     3. <u>Owners' equity</u> refers to the amount of money the owner's of the firm would have left if they sold all of the firm's assets and paid off all of the firm's liabilities. This is known as liquidating the firm.

4. <u>Revenue</u> is the value of what is received from the sale of goods and/or services plus income from other sources such as interest from bank accounts, bonds or

dividends from stock or the income from rent, etc.
a. Revenue equals Sales plus
other Income
R = S + I
5. Expenses are the costs incurred in
buying or producing the goods
and/or services sold during the
accounting period. Examples of
costs in running the business
are salaries, rent, insurance,
supplies, transportation, utilities
and taxes.

II. The Income Statement:
The Income Statement shows revenues and expenses
for a specified period of time. It demonstrates
whether the company is making a profit or not.
Sometimes it is called a profit and loss statement.
a. The equation for the Net Income Statement is:
NI = S - (C + E)
Net Income = Sales - (Costs + Expenses)
b. There are six key parts to the income
statement: revenues, costs of goods
sold, gross profit, operating expenses, gross income and net income.
1. Revenues are funds obtained
from the sales of goods,
services and products
and from royalties, rents,
interest and dividends.
2. Cost of goods sold are the
costs incurred in pro-
ducing or obtaining the
goods to be sold, e.g.
inventory.
3. Gross profit is figured by
subtracting cost of goods
sold from the net sales.
GP = NS - CGS
Gross Profit = Net Sales
- Costs of goods sold
4. Operating expenses are all
other costs not included
in the cost of goods sold
such as selling expenses
and general expenses

such as office equipment, salaries, etc.

5. <u>Gross income</u> is calculated by subtracting total expenses from total revenue.

   GI = TR - TE

   Gross Income = Total Revenue - Total Expenses

6. <u>Net income</u> is calculated by subtracting the taxes from the gross income. This is known as the bottom line which shows if the firm's activities resulted in a profit or a loss.

   NI = GI - T

   Net Income = Gross Income - Taxes

c.

INCOME STATEMENT

Sales			$150,000
Cost of Goods Sold			100,000
Gross Profit on Sales			$ 50,000
Operating Expenses			
Selling Expenses			
Salary Expense	15,000		
Advertising	3,000		
Travel & Entertainment	7,000		
Miscellaneous selling expenses	2,000		
Total Selling Expense		27,000	
General Expenses			
Office salaries	10,000		
Equipment	5,000		
Utilities	2,000		
Total General Expense		17,000	
Total Operating Expenses			44,000
Gross Income From Operations			6,000
Taxes		2,500	
Net Income From Operations			$ 3,500

III.   Statement of Changes in Financial Position:
This statement explains all changes which have occurred during the company's accounting period in its sources and uses of cash.

IV.   The Balance Sheet:
a)   The balance sheet shows the financial condition of a business at a particular moment, usually at the end of an accounting period.
1.   The fiscal period is the firm's accounting year. This does not necessarily have to coincide with the calendar year. The federal government's fiscal period is from July 1 - June 30.
b)   The balance sheet is developed from the basic accounting equation. As explained earlier we used the equation:
A - L = OE
Assets - Liabilities = Owners' Equity
However, the accounting equation is more popularly known in the following manner.
A = L + OE
Assets = Liabilities + Owners' Equity
Simply stated, if you had $100 in cash and owed someone $40, you would be worth $60. Whenever an amount is added or subtracted from one side of the accounting equation, there is required to be an opposite entry on the other side of the accounting equation. This is what is known as doulbe-entry bookkeeping.

c)

BALANCE SHEET
John's Clothing Store
December 31, 19__

ASSETS

Current Assets

Cash		$ 5,000	
Accounts Receivable	$20,000		
minus allowance for bad debts	2,000	18,000	
Inventory		25,500	
Total Current Assets			**$ 48,500**

Plant Assets

Building	$50,000	
Land	20,000	
Equipment, Furniture, etc.	10,000	
Minus depreciation on building equipment, furniture, etc.	23,000	
Total Plant Assets		**57,000**

Other Assets

Good will	1,000	
		1,000

TOTAL ASSETS	$106,500

LIABILITIES AND OWNERS' EQUITY (CAPITAL)

Current Liabilities

Accounts Payable	$27,500	
Taxes Payable	8,500	
Total Current Liabilities		**$ 36,000**

Long Term Liabilities

Mortgage on Building & Land	44,300

TOTAL LIABILITIES	80,300
JOHN JOHNSON, OWNERS' EQUITY (CAPITAL)	26,200
TOTAL LIABILITIES & OWNERS' EQUITY	106,500

V. The Accounting Cycle
   a) The first step in the accounting cycle is to
       examine source documents to show that a
       transaction occurred.
   b) The next step is the entering of the transaction
       in the accounting journal. The transaction
       will either be entered on the debit or credit
       side. The debit is the entry on the left side
       of the account, while the asset is the entry
       on the right side of the account. This was
       first used in the Italian City States during
       the period of the Renaissance during the 15th
       century.
              In accounting, debits and credits do
       not necessarily mean increases and decreases.
       Instead they refer to the column in which the
       transaction is to be entered.
   c) An increase in a liability, owners' equity or
       revenue account is recorded as a credit and
       a decrease in a liability, owners' equity or
       revenue account is recorded as a debit.

                    Debit | Credit

   d) Beginning students in accounting usually have a
       great deal of trouble in deciding whether to
       enter the transaction on the debit or credit
       side. Therefore, a memory device may help.
              "We should AID people who are Left Out
       In the Cold."

              AID – Asset increase put on
                    debit side.

              LOIC – Liabilities & Owners' Equity in-
                    crease put on credit side.

                    For decrease you reverse the
                    above statements.

e) If you prefer, there is another memory device that may help you remember what goes into the debit and credit side.

$$A = L + OE$$

One can use the saying: Did I Do Dirty = DIDD

which means

$$A = L + OE$$

Debit Side   I   D   D

Increase in Assets go in Debit Side.
Decrease in Liabilities go in Debit Side.
Decrease in Owners' Equity go in Debit Side.

One can also use the saying:

Credits can be Done by Idiots and Imbeciles = CDII

Credit Side   A = L + OE

Decrease in Assets go in Credit Side.
Increase in Liabilities go in Credit Side.
Increase in Owners' Equity go in Credit Side.

Of course, if one does not know the accounting equation, that person will have a great problem in deciding what goes where.

f) There are five key steps in the accounting cycle.
    1. Examining source documents that show transactions.
    2. Entering the transactions in the journal.
    3. Posting the transactions in the ledger.
    4. Preparing a trial balance.
    5. Preparing a financial statement.

g) In preparing the accounting cycle, it is important to be aware of the two following methods of accounting.
    1. Accrual method of accounting is a method in which income is

152

reported in the year earned and expenses are reported in the year incurred.

2. Cash method of accounting is a method in which income is reported when actually received and expenses are reported when paid.

VI. Ratios:

a) Ratios, which are developed from a firm's financial statements serve as a guide to measure the financial condition of the firm. Ratios have meaning by comparing them with established standards. By doing this, a firm can see if they have problems or not.

b) Key Ratios:

1. Short-Term Financial Ratios show the ability of a firm to pay short-term debts.

a. Current Ratio is the ratio of a firm's total current assets to its current liabilities and determines a firm's ability to meet current debts.

$$\text{Current Ratio} = \frac{\text{Current assets}}{\text{Current liabilities}}$$

$$= \frac{\$200,000}{\$100,000} = 2.0$$

This is considered to be the minimum which would enable the firm to pay its bills on time. A low ratio is an indicator that a firm might not be able to pay its future bills on time.

b. Quick Ratio or (Acid Test Ratio) measures the ability of a firm to pay its obligations without relying on the sale and collection of inventory.

$$\text{Quick Ratio} = \frac{\text{Cash + Marketable Securities + Accounts Receivables}}{\text{Current Liabilities}}$$

$$\frac{\$40,000 + 10,000 + 8,000 + 2,000}{\$55,000} = 1.09$$

The rule-of-thumb for
approximately $1.00
in quick assets is
$1.00 in current
liabilities. The quick
assets should be able
to pay the liabilities.

2. Profitability Ratios show the rate of
profitability of the firm's performance.

    a. Earnings per share is helpful
in demonstrating the
value of a firm's stock.

$$\text{Earnings per share} = \frac{\text{Net Income (from income statement)}}{\text{Common shares outstanding}}$$

$$= \frac{\$20,000}{10,000 \text{ shares}} = \$2.00 \text{ per share}$$

Whether the result is
good or bad is dependent
upon the worth of each
share of stock.

    b. Return on Investment Ratio
(ROI) is the key indi-
cator of profitability for
a firm.

$$\% \text{ of ROI} = \frac{\text{Net Profit}}{\text{Owners' Equity}}$$

$$= \frac{\$10,000}{\$100,000} = 10\%$$

The firms that are effi-
ciently using their assets
will have a relatively high
return, those with less
efficiency will have a lower return.

  c) Return on Equity is used to measure the effectiveness and profitability of the firm.

$$\text{Return on Equity} = \frac{\text{Net Income After Taxes}}{\text{Owners' Equity}}$$

$$= \frac{\$30,000}{\$145,000} = 0.206 = 20.6\%$$

d) <u>Return on Sales</u> is an indicator of the percentage on each dollar of sales.

$$\text{Return on Sales} = \frac{\text{Net Income}}{\text{Sales}} = \frac{\$10,000}{\$200,000} = .05 = 5\%$$

Therefore, the business achieved a 5% profit on each dollar of sales.

   3. <u>Activity Ratios</u> are a form of measurement which shows how efficiently a company uses its resources. These ratios are often used by potential investors to determine the probable rate of return of their investment.

      a. <u>Inventory Turnover Ratio</u> is the most used activity ratio.

         1. Measures the average number of times inventory is sold and replenished during the year.

         2. A high turnover ratio demonstrates that a small amount of money is tied up in inventory. Therefore, a high ratio shows that the company is operating in an efficient manner.

         3. One must realize that inventory turnover rates have to be compared with how the company did in previous years and how they compare with

the turnover rate of other companies in the same industry. What is an efficient rate in one industry is not necessarily an efficient rate in another industry.

$$\text{Inventory Turnover Ratio} = \frac{\text{Cost of Goods Sold}}{\text{Average Inventory}}$$

$$= \frac{\$100,000}{(\$15,000 + \$25,000)/2} = 5 \text{ times}$$

The average inventory is the average of inventory value on January 1, and December 31, of the same year.

4. Financial Norms:
   Certain questions are usually asked in determining financial norms.
   a. What are the norms of the industry?
   b. How are similar firms doing?
   c. How is the firm doing as compared with its past performance?
   d. What can the firm expect to achieve in the future?

VII. Budgeting:
    a) A budget is a company's financial plan showing how resources will be used in terms of dollars, hours, units, etc.
    b) Budgets are developed in order to achieve company objectives.
    c) Budgets are used for controlling operations so that management can identify problem areas.
    d) Budgets are a standard for measuring a firm's overall performance.
    e) Budgets show how the firm's funds will be used and the sources from which the firm will obtain the funds.
    f) Different types of budgets are:
        1. <u>Sales budgets</u> which has the purpose of estimating how many items will be sold and the revenue that will be received from the sales.
        2. <u>Production budget</u> is used to estimate the number of items needed to fill the sales orders and maintain the necessary inventory.
        3. <u>Cost-of-goods-sold budget</u> is used to figure the cost for the goods sold. This includes the cost of labor, materials, taxes, insurance, energy, etc.

VIII. Methods of Recording Revenue:
    a) Business run on an <u>accrual basis</u> records all sales revenue in the year the the sales are made. This is done even if the purchaser does not pay until the next year. Expenses are recorded in the year in which the corresponding revenue is reported. The revenue and the expenses must be reported in the same year for tax purposes.
    b) Business run on a <u>cash basis</u> records the revenues only when the money from the sales is actually received. Expenses are recorded when they are actually received.

IX. Depreciation:
    a) <u>Depreciation</u> is an estimated decline in the value of an asset due to that asset being used up or suffering from wear and tear. Depreciating an asset over a number of years serves to spread out the cost of that particular asset.

1. Depreciation is an estimation that is never exact. There are various accounting methods of depreciation such as sum-of-digits method and the fixed-percentage-of-diminishing-value method.

QUESTIONS FOR REVIEW AND DISCUSSION

1. What is accounting?

2. How are assets different from liabiltiies?

3. Explain the income statement.

4. What is the purpose of the balance sheet?

5. Explain the accounting cycle.

6. Explain:

    a) Current Ratio

    b) Quick Ratio

    c) Accounting Equation

    d) Revenue

    e) Expenses

    f) Owners' Equity

    g) Return on Equity

    h) Return on Sales

    i) Inventory Turnover Ratio

    j) Depreciation.

7. Explain the importance of the different types of budgets.

XXIV

MONEY AND BANKING

I. <u>Money</u> is any type of object that can be used as a medium of exchange for goods and/or services.
    a) Money must possess four characteristics:
        1. Portability - it should be light and easy to handle.
        2. Divisibility - can easily be divided into smaller portions with a fixed value for each unit. In the United States, a dollar can be exchanged for 100 pennies, 20 nickels, 10 dimes, 4 quarters, 2 half-dollars or a combination of these coins.
        3. Durability - the money will last. It will not evaporate due to excessive use.
        4. Stability - the value of the money does not change too rapidly.
    b) <u>Liquidity</u> is the ability of an asset to be converted into currency in a short period of time.
        1. <u>Demand deposits</u> permit a person to withdraw his money without prior notice to the bank.
        2. <u>Time deposits</u> require that notice be given to the bank before a person is allowed to withdraw his money.
    c) Composition of the United States Money Supply:
        1. <u>Currency</u> consists of two of the components of the United States money supply; coins and paper money.
        2. <u>Demand deposits</u> is the name for checking accounts. This is a promise by the bank to immediately pay the depositor any amount that he has in his checking account.
        3. <u>NOW or negotiable order of withdrawal accounts</u> are interest-bearing checking accounts which can be opened in almost all banks.

4. Super NOW accounts are similar to the NOW account except that it pays a higher interest rate. A super NOW account also requires a minimum balance.
5. Share draft accounts are used by depositors in a credit union. It allows the credit union depositor to receive interest and to write drafts which are basically the same as checks.

d) Near-Money:
1. Near-money are assets which are nearly as liquid as checking accounts. However, they cannot be directly used as a medium of exchange. An example of near-money is a time deposit. A time deposit is a savings account but the bank must receive prior notice from the depositor before a withdrawal. If prior notice is not given, the bank is permitted to assess a penalty for the early withdrawal.
    a. Other examples of near-money are:
        1. Money-market mutual funds.
        2. Bank money-market accounts.
        3. Government bonds.

e) The Money Supply:
1. In order for money to be a medium of exchange or a store of value, buyers and sellers must give it the same value.
    a. The value of money depends upon its supply. The more money in circulation, the less value the money has. The less money in circulation, the more value the money has.

b. If more money is in cir-
culation, there will
be <u>inflation</u> (a rise
in <u>prices</u>). This occurs because the
value of the dollar
drops and the con-
sumer has more money
to spend on goods.
if the consumer has
more money to spend
on goods, there will
be a rise in prices
because the increase
in money will force
the prices upward.
        In addition,
sellers will raise their
prices because they
will have to pay
higher prices for
labor and materials.
For example, the cost
of a house will in-
crease because the
builder will have to
pay more for labor
and supplies.

2. <u>M-1</u> is a measure of the money supply and refers to only very
liquid forms of money such as:
a. Currency
b. Demand deposits
c. NOW accounts
d. Super-NOW accounts
e. Share draft accounts
f. Traveler's checks.

3. <u>M-2</u> is a measure of the money supply that includes M-1 plus near-
money such as:
a. Time deposits
b. U. S. government bonds
c. Money-market mutual
    funds
d. Bank money-market ac-
    counts.

II. Financial Intermediaries:
- a) A <u>financial intermediary</u> is one who receives funds from one source and then lends to another source at a profitable rate of interest. For example, these include banks, insurance companies and pension funds.
- b) <u>Nondepository intermediaries</u> are financial organizations such as pension funds and insurance companies.
    1. <u>Pension funds</u> receive contributions from employees and employers and put the money into a myriad of investments in order to finance the retirement benefits of those belonging to the pension fund.
    2. <u>Insurance companies</u> receive premiums from policyholders and pay if a loss occurs for which the insurance was purchased.
        a. Insurance companies invest much of the premium money into such areas as real estate, stocks, etc.
    3. <u>Commercial finance companies</u> and <u>consumer finance companies</u> are also nondepository institutions who lend money to businesses and consumers at a higher rate of interest than a bank.
        a. These companies usually lend to those people who cannot get a bank loan.
        b. Commercial finance companies lend money to businesses.
        c. Consumer finance companies lend small amounts of money to individuals for non-commercial uses, e.g. house appliances, vacations, etc.
- c) <u>Depositary intermediaries</u> are financial institutions that receive deposits. These include commercial banks, savings and loan associations, mutual savings banks and credit unions.

1. <u>Commercial banks</u> are privately owned profit-seeking institutions that accept demand deposits. Checks may be drawn on the account.
    a. The main function of commercial banks is to provide loans for businesses.
    b. Commercial banks also permit depositors to have time deposits such as savings accounts and certificates of deposit (CD's).
    c. Commercial banks also issue credit cards.
    d. Deposits in commercial banks are insured up to $100,000 by the Federal Deposit Insurance Corporation (FDIC), an agency of the U. S. government.
    e. Commercial banks carry most of the load of the American banking system. There are approximately 15,000 commercial banks in the United States.
    f. Commercial banks are depository intermediaries.
    g. Many commercial banks provide trust services. They manage an individual's investments or estate in return for a fee.
    h. Many commercial banks also provide help in the conducting of international business.
        1. They issue <u>letters of credit</u> which is a bank's written promise, issued on behalf of a

purchaser, to
pay a partic-
ular company
a specified
amount of
money if cer-
tain conditions
are fulfilled.
For example,
a U.S. com-
pany pays its
bank, Chase,
to pay an
Italian firm a
specified
amount of
money if cer-
tain conditions
are met. In
this situation,
the bank has
to be shown
documents
that certain
goods were
shipped.

2. Banker's accept-
ance is when
a purchaser
pays his bank
to issue a
written prom-
ise to pay a
foreign firm a
specified
amount of
money by a
specified date.

2. Savings and loan associations and
mutual savings banks have as
their main function the lending
of money to people in order to
buy homes. Home loan mort-
gages are given to people in the
local communities.

a. These banks can provide
checking account ser-
vices for their custom-
ers.

　　　　　b. The deposits are insured
　　　　　　　by the Federal
　　　　　　　Savings and Loan In-
　　　　　　　surance Corporation
　　　　　　　(FSLIC), an agency
　　　　　　　of the federal govern-
　　　　　　　ment. The deposits
　　　　　　　are insured up to
　　　　　　　$100,000.
　　　3. Credit unions are a nonprofit savings
　　　　　　and loan association. They are
　　　　　　owned by members of a firm, or
　　　　　　members of a club or organiza-
　　　　　　tion.
　　　　　　　a. Deposits are insured by
　　　　　　　　the National Credit
　　　　　　　　Union Administration.

III. The Federal Reserve System:
　　　　At the head of the American banking system is the
Federal Reserve System (known as "The Fed" or the
FRS). The Federal Reserve System functions as the
United States' central bank. In most nations, the cen-
tral bank is either owned or operated by the government.
In the United States, the central bank, which is the
Federal Reserve System, is in charge of managing the
U. S. monetary policy, regulating the commercial bank-
ing system and controlling the money supply. The Fed
also oversees the United States' international financial
policy. The main purpose of the Federal Reserve System
is to control the money supply of the United States.
　　　　The Federal Reserve System was established by
Congress in 1913 by the passing of the Federal Reserve
Act. The purpose of this act was to attempt to regulate
the financial system of the country by aiding and supervising banking policies.
　　　a) Organization of the Federal Reserve System:
　　　　　1. At the top of the Fed is the Chairman
　　　　　　　who is appointed by the President of
　　　　　　　the United States.
　　　　　2. Below the Chairman, is the Board of
　　　　　　　Governors, which gives general
　　　　　　　direction to the twelve Federal Re-
　　　　　　　serve District Banks. The Board of
　　　　　　　Governors consist of seven members,
　　　　　　　appointed by the President and ap-
　　　　　　　pointed to 14 year terms.

3. Below the Board of Governors are the
12 Federal Reserve Banks:
    a. There is one Federal Reserve
       Bank (FRB) for each
       district.
    b. Each FRB is owned by the
       commercial banks located
       in its district. These
       banks keep a percentage
       of their deposits with the
       area Federal Reserve
       Bank.
    c. The FRB's attempt to make
       the U. S. financial sys-
       tem run smoothly.
    d. The FRB's issue currency,
       sell U. S. Savings bonds
       and supervise the trans-
       fer of money.
    e. There are 9 directors on
       each FRB. Three of the
       directors must be bank-
       ers, three must be busi-
       ness people and three
       are appointed by the
       Board of Governors of
       the Federal Reserve Sys-
       tem to represent the
       interests of the general
       public.
b) The Fed's Regulation of the Money Supply:
    1. The Fed manages the money supply in
       the United States. As previously
       stated, this is their primary function.
        a. The Federal Open Market
           Committee (FOMC) per-
           forms open-market oper-
           ations in order to control
           the money supply. The
           FOMC purchases and
           sells U. S. government
           securities (U. S.
           Treasury notes, U. S.
           Treasury bills and U. S.
           government bonds) so
           that there could either
           be an increase or a de-
           crease in the monetary

funds available for lend-
ing by member banks.

    b. In order to increase the
money supply, the Fed
buys U. S. securities
from member banks. The
bank is then credited
with the money that the
Fed paid for the secur-
ities. Therefore, the
bank has more money to
lend and the money sup-
ply increases. To put it
more simply, if the Fed
buys securities, it in-
creases the amount of
money that the member
banks have to lend to
their customers.

    c. If the Fed desires to de-
crease the money supply,
it sells U. S. securities.
If the Fed sells secur-
ities, it decreases the
amount of money banks
have available to lend to
its customers. This is
because member banks
must buy the securities
that the Fed sells. When
the member banks are
buying the securities,
they are turning money
over to the Fed and this
money is therefore not
available for lending to
customers.

2. The Fed also measures the money supply.
This is done every week and is the
M-1 and M-2 which was discussed
earlier.

    a. If the Fed knows the amount
of money available, it
can use whatever eco-
nomic tools it possesses
in order to try to regu-
late the money supply.

3. Reserve requirements are set by the Fed.
They determine the percentage of

deposits that a member bank must retain in cash. For example, banks make money by lending money for interest. The more money a bank lends, the more interest they receive. The interst is hopefully their profit. If a bank has ten million dollars in deposits and the Fed states that they must retain 10% of their deposits, that means that the bank can lend out nine million dollars.

If the Fed decides to increase the reserve requirement to 15%, that would mean that the bank only has $8,500,000 to lend. Obviously, this decreases the amount of funds available to lend and this may cool down the economy and slow down inflation.

If, on the other hand, the Fed decides to decrease the reserve requirement to 5%, that would mean that the bank has $9,500,000 to lend. Obviously, this increases the amount of funds available to lend and this may heat up the economy and increase inflation.

4. Discount rate is the interest rate that the Federal Reserve District Bank charges on its loans to member banks.

If the Fed decides to lower the discount rate, the member banks will probably borrow more money and therefore have more money to lend to their customers and this might stimulate a slow economy.

If the Fed decides to raise the the discount rate, the member banks will probably borrow less money and therefore have less money to lend to their customers and this might slow down an overheated economy.

5. Credit controls are used by the FRS to help control the economy.

    a. The FRS also controls the margin requirements which sets the amount of stock one can buy on credit. If the FRS raised the margin requirements, it reduces the quantity of stock one may be able to buy on credit. Therefore, this method can be used to cool off the economy and reduce inflation.

6. The Federal Reserve also regulates member banks in the use of automated teller machines (ATM), electronic funds transfer (EFT) and check clearing.

7. Because the Federal Reserve System assists the member banks in a variety of banking services, it is known as a banker's bank.

QUESTIONS FOR REVIEW AND DISCUSSION

1. Describe the functions of money.

2. Explain the characteristics of money.

3. How is M-1 different from M-2?

4. How are depository intermediaries different from non-depository intermediaries?

5. It has been said that "commercial banks are the workhorses of the American banking system. Explain.

6. Explain the functions of the Federal Reserve System.

7. How does the Federal Reserve System regulate the money supply?

XXV

STOCKS AND BONDS

I. Security (a certificate of ownership) exchanges specialize in bringing together those people who wish to buy and sell stocks and bonds.
    a) A <u>share of stock</u> represents ownership in a company.
    b) <u>Common stock</u> represents ownership in a corporation. Owners of common stock have voting privileges, have a fixed dividend and in case of liquidation, the common stockholders get paid last, after bondholders and preferred stockholders.
    c) <u>Preferred stockholders</u> do not have voting rights in the affairs of the corporation but in case of liquidation they get paid after the bondholders but before the common stockholders.
    d) <u>Asked price</u> is the lowest price one will accept for a security (stock) at a particular time.
    e) <u>Bid price</u> is the highest price an individual will pay for a security (stock) at a particular time.

II. People buy securities for a variety of reasons.
    a) <u>Investment</u> - stock is purchased with the intent of being held for a relatively long period of time with the hope that the value of the stock will appreciate over a period of time.
    b) <u>Speculation</u> - is when one buys stock with the intent of selling the stock within a short period of time with the hope of making a quick profit.

III. The market place for trading stocks is known as the <u>stock exchange</u>.
    a) To become a member of the <u>New York Stock Exchange</u>, one must purchase a <u>seat</u> on the exchange.
    b) All stocks that have been approved for trading on organized securities (stock) exchanges are called <u>listed stock</u>.
    c) Organized stock exchanges are:
        1. New York Stock Exchange (NYSE) known as "The Big Board"
        2. American Stock Exchange (AMEX)

3. Regional stock exchanges - e.g. Chicago, Denver, etc.
4. Foreign exchanges - Tokyo (largest exchange in world), London, Paris, Geneva, etc.

d) Over-The-Counter (OTC) market trades stocks that are not listed on the various stock exchanges.

e) Stock averages are an index of stock prices.
1. Dow Jones Industrial Average (DJIA) is determined from the market prices of 30 industrial stocks.
2. Standard & Poor's Composite Index (S & P) is determined by computing 500 selected stocks.
3. New York Stock Exchange Index is determined by including all of its listed stocks.

IV. Buyers and sellers of stock place their orders through brokers.

a) Full-service broker - a broker who not only buys and sells for his or her clients but also advises them.

b) Discount broker - is a broker who buys and sells for a client but does not advise them. A discount broker usually charges a client less than a full-service broker.

c) Most stock transactions usually take a few minutes to complete.
1. In general, the larger the transaction, the lower is the broker's commission rate.
a. Round lot transactions are stock trades that are in lots of 100 shares of stock.
b. Odd lot transactions are stock trades in lots which are less than 100 shares of stock.

d) Buying on margin means that the purchaser of a stock pays for a certain percentage of the purchase and obtains credit through the stock-broker for the balance.
1. Stocks which are bought on margin are held by the brokerage

firm until full payment is
made by the buyer. If the
price of the stock drops a
particular amount, the
brokerage house will request
the buyer to put up more
margin (money) to cover the
decline in the stock.

e) Selling short is when a seller borrows money
from a brokerage house. He then agrees
to sell shares of the stock that he
doesn't own yet at a certain price. The
short seller believes that in the future,
the price of the stock will decline.
Therefore, he can buy the stock at a
lower price. The seller then hopes that
the price of the stock will go up and
therefore the seller will make a profit.

f) Open order is an order by the buyer to the
stock broker to purchase stock at a
specific price but without a time limit on
the purchase.

g) Bull market is when stock prices move upward.

h) Bear market is when stock prices move
downward.

V. Bonds:
a) A bond is a certificate of indebtedness. A bond
represents the debt of the issuing company,
municipality, state, local or federal agency.

1. Registered bond - is one in which
the name of the owner of the
bond is on the bond. The owner's name is registered with the
issuer of the bond and interest
is paid to him.

2. Bearer bond - has no name on it and
the interest payments are made
to the person who holds the
bond.

3. Mortgage bond - is secured by the
real property of the issuing
organization.

4. Income bond - pays interest only if
there is enough income.

5. Convertible bond - can be exchanged
for shares of common stock.

172

6. Collateral trust bond - secured by stock owned by the company.
7. Equipment trust bond - the money from the bond is used to buy equipment which then serves as security for the bond.
8. Debenture bond - is secured by the good name and credit reputation of the company issuing the bond.
9. Municipal bonds - bonds which are issued by state and local governments and backed by taxation or other revenue.
10. U. S. Government securities - this is when the federal government borrows money from the public. These securities are U. S. Savings bonds, Treasury bonds, Treasury notes and Treasury bills. They are backed by the full faith and credit on the U. S. government.

VI. Mutual Funds, Commodities and Options:
   a) A mutual fund is an investment company which is managed by a group of professional managers. These companies have fulltime managers who are very knowledgeable about stocks, bonds and other types of investments. In a mutual fund, individual investors pool their financial resources and the professional managers invest the combined financial resources into a variety of investments. Most of the investments are based on the philosophy of spreading the risk. The mutual fund will usually invest in a variety of stocks, bonds and other investment instruments with the belief that if one of the stocks, bonds, etc., fails, the investor's damage will be limited because there is a very small chance of all stocks, bonds, etc., failing.
      1. Mutual funds may be load (a commission is charged to the buyer of the fund) or no load (no commission is charged to the buyer).
   b) Commodities are contracts which are commitments to purchase a specified amount of a commodity such as gold, cotton, wheat, pork-bellies

at a particular time in the future. It is also
known as the futures market.
     1.   These contracts are traded on the
           secondary market.
     2.   When one deals in future contracts
           one should be very careful be-
           cause it is an extremely risky
           business. If you are not fully
           cognizant of the ramifications of
           trading in futures, do not try it
           without sufficient qualified and
           responsible assistance.

c) Options are when one pays for the privilege to
     either buy or sell at a specific price a hun-
     dred shares of a certain common stock within
     a specific period of time.
           1. Calls are option contracts that give
                the owners of the calls the right
                to purchase 100 shares of a
                particular stock at a predeter-
                mined date and at a predeter-
                mined price.
                  a. The buyer of a call tries
                     to take advantage of
                     a rise in the price
                     of a common stock
                     above what he con-
                     tracted to purchase
                     the stock for. If the
                     buyer does not exer-
                     cise his right to pur-
                     chase the stock, all
                     he loses is the price
                     of the call which
                     usually averages
                     about 10% of the
                     price of the stock.
           2. Puts are option contracts that give
                the owner of the put the right to
                 sell 100 shares of a certain com-
                mon stock within a specified peri-
                od of time.

VII. Sources of financial information:
     a) Magazines such as Barrons, Industry Week,
        Forbes, Business Week and Fortune.
     b) Newspapers such as New York Times, Wall Street
        Journal and industry papers such as Women's
        Wear Daily and the Daily News Record.

c) Other sources of financial information are radio, television, company's prospectus, company's annual reports, etc.

VIII. Government Regulation of Securities (stocks)
a) Until the depression of the 1930s the United States government did very little regulation of the securities market. However, because of the great amount of watered stock and situations of fraud during the 1920s many people felt that there had to be some regulation over the trading of securities. Since the 1930s there has been a growing amount of government regulation of the securities industry. Among the key acts are:
1. The Securities Act of 1933 stated that issues of public securities must give the public information about the company's financial situation, its management and operation.
2. The Securities Exchange Act (1934) was passed in order to establish the Securities Exchange Commission (SEC) in order to enforce securities laws passed by the federal government.
3. The Public Utility Holding Company Act (1936) gave the SEC the power to regulate public utility companies.
4. The Trust Indenture Act (1939) stated that corporate bonds which are offered to the public must be registered with the Securities Exchange Commission.
5. The Investment Company Act (1940) put mutual funds under regulation by the SEC.
6. The Securities Act of 1964 put over-the-counter (OTC) stock under the control of the SEC. This act enlarged upon the Maloney Act of 1938 in which the over-the-counter market regulated itself.
7. The Insider Trading Sanctions Act (1984) put financial penalties and prison sentences for insider trading. It was this act that

175

led to the sentencing of a number of Wall Street big-shots to prison and large fines. The SEC was given the authority to enforce this act.

QUESTIONS FOR REVIEW AND DISCUSSION

1. How is preferred stock different from common stock?

2. Why do people buy securities?

3. How is a full-service broker different from a discount broker?

4. Why does one decide to sell short?

5. How is a debenture bond different from a mortgage bond?

6. Why would people buy mutual funds instead of individual stocks or bonds?

7. Why are options considered advantageous to certain investors?

8. Why can buying on margin be a large risk?

9. How has the federal government regulated the trading of securities?

XXVI

FINANCIAL MANAGEMENT

I. The Role of the Financial Manager
    a) To identify and handle the financial needs of the company.
        1. Identify short term working capital (money) needs.
            a. The financial manager oversees the collection of bills from the firm's customers so that cash is not tied up unnecessarily.
            b. Identify long term capital (money) needs.
    b) To identify, evaluate and select from various sources of funds
        1. Debt sources - either long or short term sources.
        2. Equity sources - either long or short term sources.
    c) To protect the company's resources while trying to maximize the company's return on investment.

II. Working Capital Needs
    a) Working Capital is also known as current assets (cash or assets that can be converted into cash within a short period of time - one year or less). Working capital is necessary to provide the finances for carrying out the current operations of the firm, such as;
        1. Current cash needs
        2. Needs of inventory
        3. For sales on account - this is accounts receivable (when you sell an item or a service but have not received payment for it).
    b) The financial manager has to determine the pros and cons of maintaining large amounts of current assets (working capital) in inventories (stock, supplies, etc.) and receivables (money owed to the firm) measured against the cost of acquiring capital.
    c) The financial manager must decide whether to keep large amounts of money on hand or

invest it in new equipment, facilities, etc.
The financial manager has to make the following kinds of choices.

Sometimes, a firm has a great deal of
extra cash but the financial manager does
not wish to put that money into plant or
equipment. He or she might then put the
cash to use by investing in marketable (easy
to sell) securities that will yield sufficient
interest. The securities in which financial
managers usually invest are bank certificates
of deposit, large corporations commercial
paper and U. S. Treasury bills, notes, bonds
and certificates.

III. Fixed Assets
   a) Fixed assets are assets that are long term (more
       than one year). Some examples of fixed
       assets are property, plant, heavy equipment
       and machinery.
          1. Capital expenditures are the long-
              term investments that a firm
              makes in buying such fixed
              assets as property, plant and
              heavy equipment. In evaluating
              whether to make a capital expen-
              diture, the financial manager
              must determine:
                a. How much will it cost?
                b. How much income will it
                   generate?
                c. How long will the invest-
                   ment last?
                d. What are our competitors
                   doing?
                e. Are the benefits of the
                   investment worth the
                   cost?
                f. Maybe there are greater
                   benefits in leasing?
                   1. Leasing is
                     used as an
                     alternative
                     to long-
                     term capital
                     investment.
                     Leasing is
                     when you
                     use an item

for a peri-
od of time
for a spe-
cific price.
Many
managers
find that
leasing re-
duces the
outstanding
debt of the
firm, gives
some de-
fense
against
obsolescence
and in addi-
tion, may
provide
some tax
advantages.

IV. Equity Financing
    a) Equity financing is achieved by increasing the
        ownership of the company by selling shares
        of stock. It does not require that there be
        fixed payments to the investors and the firm
        has a choice of whether it wishes to pay
        dividends or not.
            1. Since there is no fixed maturity date,
               equity financing can relieve a
               certain amount of pressure on the
               firm.
            2. Many firms do not like equity finan-
               cing because the selling of addi-
               tional shares of stock gives
               control to new owners. In addi-
               tion, more people can then share
               in the profits and according to
               current tax-law, dividends are
               not deductible.

V. Debt Financing
    a) Debt financing is the borrowing of funds to fi-
        nance long term capital projects. In order
        to do this, the firm sells bonds. A bond is
        a certificate of indebtedness which is really
        a promissory note to repay a loan.

1. Debt financing is cheaper than equity financing.
2. When a firm borrows money, it does not give up power or control as it does in equity financing.
3. Interest (charge paid for borrowing money) must be paid to the creditors (the one who lends you money) even if you do not make a profit. However, the interest is tax deductible.
4. Debt financing entails a fixed maturity date.
5. If debt financing is too heavy it can make the company look to be on shaky ground.

VI. Short-term sources of financing
   a) Trade credit is made up of "open book" accounts. The seller ships the goods and the buyer receives a bill (invoice) giving him a certain amount of time to pay. This chould be ten days, twenty days, thirty days, sixty days, etc.
   b) Commercial paper is a promissory note given by a large company agreeing to pay back the money within a short period of time. These are usually called debentures (no security is offered except the good name of the company).
   c) Commercial banks are sources for financing. This could involve getting a line of credit or a revolving credit account. It could also consist of receiving a variety of loan terms depending upon whether loans are secured or not the general credit of the borrower.

VII. Long term sources of financing
   a) The corporation can obtain long term sources of financing in the following ways:
      1. Retained earnings - putting profits back into the company instead of distributing them.
      2. Common stock
      3. Preferred stock
      4. Bonds.
   b) Noncorporate firms can obtain long term sources of financing in the following ways:
      1. Personal funds of the owner

2. Retaining profits and putting them
back into the company
3. Bringing in new partners
4. Borrowing from banks
5. Borrowing from private sources -
venture capitalists, friends, etc.

VIII. Exceptional financial arrangements
a) Methods for expansion and combination
1. Merger - the combining of two firms
where the dominant firm takes over
the weaker one.
2. Amalgamation is when two firms unite
into one. This is a consolidation
similar to a merger.
3. Holding company - is when another company is created and this company
holds the majority of shares in another company and therefore maintains control.
b) Recapitalization is when voluntary changes in
capital structure are made in order to adjust
to changing business conditions.
1. This can include changes in the type
of preferred stock, changes in
the maturity date of the bonds
or the yield on the bonds.
c) Bankruptcy occurs when a firm is unable to meet
its financial obligations.
1. When liabilities are greater than
assets, a firm is said to be in
bankruptcy. The firm legally
files for bankruptcy.
2. A firm is in voluntary bankruptcy
when it files in the federal
courts and makes it assets available to its creditors.
3. Many times, creditors take a debtor
into the federal court and have
him declared bankrupt. This is
called an involuntary bankruptcy.
If a bankruptcy petition is grant-
ed to the creditors by the federal
courts, they get control of the
firm's assets and divide them
among the creditors.
d) Reorganization is an involuntary action that occurs if a firm has very serious financial
problems. The business is then reorganized

under court supervision in order to protect
the interests of the creditors. This is known
as Chapter 11.

QUESTIONS FOR REVIEW AND DISCUSSION

1. Explain the role of the financial manager.

2. Why is working capital important for the firm?

3. What should the financial manager consider before making
   capital expenditures?

4. How is equity financing different from debt financing?

5. How can a company obtain short-term financing?

6. Which are the best sources of long-term financing? Why?

7. Why should a firm decide to recapitalize?

8. How is voluntary bankruptcy different from involuntary
   bankruptcy?

XXVII

TAXES AND BUSINESS

Taxes are placed on individuals and businesses for the purpose of raising revenue (money) for the governments to meet its expenditures. Federal, state and local governments place taxes on individuals and businesses in order to increase revenue. However, many people in the United States presently believe that one of the main objectives of taxation is to redistribute wealth from those who produce and have to those who do not produce. Others take the position that it is only fair and proper for those who earn more to pay a higher percentage of their earnings than those who earn less. It is obvious that as long as there is taxation there will be controversy.

I. History of Taxation in the United States:
    a) Beginning in 1789 when Washington became the first President of the United States, until the Civil War, over 90% of the revenue was raised by customs receipts. Therefore, great emphasis was placed on the taxing of imported goods. Other revenue was raised by the sale of public lands.
    b) The Civil War led to the growth of a variety of taxes including the first income tax which was put into effect in 1862. This was a progressive tax of 3% up $10,000 and 5% on all income over $10,000. As the Civil War progressed the rates were raised in 1864. After the Civil War the income tax and inheritance taxes that were passed during that period were reduced and dropped altogether by 1867.
    c) Though the income tax was repealed in 1867 there was great demand for an income tax to be installed. Labor groups and farmers in the 1880's and 1890's were in favor of making a progressive income tax a permanent part of American law. The business interests were strongly against the imposition of an income tax and their philosophy was dominant in the Republican Party. The philosophy of labor and the farmers was put forth by the Populist Party in the form of favoring a graduated income tax. The Populist position became part of the Democratic Party philosophy. In the ensuing battle the labor groups and the farmers were victorious. In

1894, as part of the Wilson-Gorham Tariff
Act, an income tax was passed. This tax
was set at 2% on individual and corporation
net income with a $4,000 exemption for the
individual. Obviously, during thei period of
time, it was a tax on the wealthiest 1% of the
population. Of course, this had to be fought
out in the courts to determine if an income
tax was constitutional. This was because
many Americans believed that Article I Section 2 clause 3 and Section 9 clause 4 required that direct taxes shall be apportioned
among the states of the union according to
their population and therefore the income tax
was a direct tax and was unconstitutional because there wasn't any apportionment. The
United States Supreme Court in Pollock vs.
Farmers' Loan and Trust Company (1895)
held that the income tax was unconstitutional.

Therefore, an amendment to the Constitution had to be passed. This amendment
was passed in 1913 and stated that "The
Congress shall have power to lay and collect
taxes on incomes, from whatever sources
derived, without apportionment among the
several states, and without regard to any
census or enumeration." (For further information on the development of the income tax
see Surry, Stanley, Warren, William C.,
McDaniel, Paul R. and Ault, Hugh J., Federal Income Taxation: Cases and Materials,
Mineola, N. Y., Foundation Press, 1972,
pgs. 1-27.)

II. Types of Taxes
    a) Proportional taxation is where the rate of tax-
ation stays constant regardless of how much
income an individual has. For example, if
an individual earns $100,000 per year and is
taxed at 10%, that person will pay $10,000 in
taxes. If an individual earns $20,000 per
year, the individual is also taxed on a 10%
basis and he will pay $2,000 per year in
taxes.
    b) Regressive taxation is where the rate of taxation
decreases as an individual earns more income.
For example, if an individual earns $20,000
per year he might be taxed at 20%, which
would mean that he would pay $4,000 in taxes.

184

If an individual earned $100,000 he would be taxed at a rate of 10% and therefore would pay $10,000 in taxes. Simply put, the more money you earn, the less percentage in taxes you pay.

c) <u>Progressive taxation</u> is where the rate of taxation increases as an individual earns more income. For example, if you earn $20,000 per year, you would be taxed at 10% which means you would pay $2,000 in taxes. If you earned $100,000 per year you would be taxed at 35% which means you pay $35,000 in taxes. The more money you earn, the higher percentage of taxes you pay.

III. Taxes Influence Business Decisions
    a) State and local taxes play a part in determining the location of a business facility.
        1. Some states and localities will give businesses tax abatements in order to attract companies to their area.
        2. Businesses also have to consider the tax rates of the states and local areas before deciding where to locate.
        3. Sales taxes, manufacturers and retailers excise taxes and other kinds of taxes play a large part in determining business decisions.
    b) Federal taxation also affects business decisions.
        1. Whether a business incorporates or not is sometimes affected by the double taxation of corporate income given to individuals as dividends.
        2. If a company sells bonds in order to raise funds this will mean that they have to pay interest and this will result in a decrease of taxable profits. However, if the company decides to sell stock, they may have to pay dividends and this is an after-tax distribution of the company's profits.
        3. Companies also make decisions on depreciation, writing off bad debts, payment of executives, research and development and other issues, based in great part on federal tax consequences.

4. Tariffs also influence whether a producer should make goods in foreign lands or make the goods in the United States.
5. Corporate taxes affect business decisions in determining whether to build a plant in the United States or to build a plant overseas.

QUESTIONS FOR REVIEW AND DISCUSSION

1. Why does the government tax businesses and individuals?

2. Why was the Civil War so instrumental in the development of the idea of the income tax?

3. Which type of income tax (proportional, regressive, progressive) do you believe to be the most equitable?

4. Should business carry a heavy tax burden? Why?

5. Should state or local communities use tax policy to encourage or discourage business from coming to or leaving their areas?

PART FIVE

OTHER ASPECTS OF BUSINESS

XXVIII

SMALL BUSINESS AND FRANCHISING

The Small Business Act of 1953 said that "a <u>small business</u> concern shall be deemed to be one which is independently owned and operated and which is not dominant in its field of operation."

Small business ownership has long been a tradition in American society. Small businesses have provided the means by which many individuals have been able to achieve financial, creative, independent and self-satisfying success.

I. What is small business?
   a) A small business is when an entrepreneur (usually he or she is the owner-manager of a small business) takes on the financial risk of starting up a business.
   b) A small business is one that is independently owned and operated and is not a major force in its industry.
      1. Capital is given to the business by one person or a small group of individuals.
      2. The size of the company is small compared to other companies in the industry.
   c) A small business is one whose activities are usually retail or wholesale, construction and production.
   d) An <u>entrepreneur</u> is one who risks his own finances to organize a business in return for a profit.

II. Why people go into small business:
   a) Independence.
   b) Chance for big profits.
   c) Chance to develop their own ideas.
   d) Self-actualization.

III. What type of person is the entrepreneur?
   a) Self-motivated.
   b) Commitment to the enterprise.
   c) A strong sense of responsibility.
   d) Self-disciplined.
   e) Willingness to work very hard.
   f) Desire to be independent.
   g) Perseverance.
   h) Does not get discouraged easily.

i) Willing to take calculated risks.
j.) An action-oriented individual.
k) A strong desire to succeed.
l) Sets objectives and wishes to achieve them.
m) A high degree of energy.

IV. Key terms
   a) <u>Small Business Administration (SBA)</u> - an agency of the federal government which helps small businesses with loans, training, publications and additional help for minority businesses.
   b) <u>Venture Capitalist</u> - a person who looks for new areas in which to invest money.

V. What type of management should a small business have?
   a) A small business manager should understand the principle of management the same as a manager in a big firm. However, the small business manager has a greater variety of responsibilities and usually his own capital tied up in the venture. Therefore, the small business manager has to be adept at a variety of managerial endeavors but must not be afraid to call upon expert help when he is faced with a situation outside his area of knowledge.

VI. Basic Plan for starting a new business (Based on pamphlets put out by the Small Business Administration).
   a) Determine what kind of business you are in.
   b) What goods and services do you provide?
   c) Determine where your market is.
      1. Who will buy your product or service?
      2. Why will they buy it?
   d) Determine the competition you will encounter.
   e) Develop a sales strategy.
   f) Develop plans of production, construction servicing and merchandising.
   g) Develop plans for financial analysis and data.
   h) How will the business be organized and what kind of personnel will you employ?
   i) Cash flow and break-even analysis.
   j) A system of management controls must be developed.
   k) A method of revising plans to fit changing conditions should be designed.
   l) Putting plans into action.

VII.   Planning is very important in starting a new business.
        It should be noted that over 250,000 new businesses
        are started in the U. S. each year and about 75% of
        these businesses fail within the first five years.
        If people would plan more carefully there would
        probably be less business failures.

VIII.   Advantages and disadvantages of a small business.

<u>Advantages</u>

(1) Can respond to
    change quickly
(2) Decisions are made
    faster
(3) Ideas can be tried
    more quickly
(4) Closer personal
    relationship with
    customers
(5) Closer personal
    relationship with
    suppliers
(6) A successful busi-
    ness venture
    brings about a
    great deal of
    self-actualiza-
    tion to the
    entrepreneur
(7) Independence
(8) Ability to adapt
    to local needs.

<u>Disadvantages</u>

(1) Lack of expertise
    in vital areas
    of management
(2) Lack of capital
    and various
    problems be-
    cause of diffi-
    culty in attract-
    ing adequate
    financing
(3) Problems in get-
    ting qualified
    employees
(4) The owner-
    manager can
    work extreme-
    ly hard and
    still lose in
    the end.
(5) High degree of
    risk
(6) Personal stress
(7) Very long hours
    of work
(8) Risk of your own
    funds.

IX.   Franchising
       In <u>franchising</u>, one company (called the franchisor)
           licenses another company (franchisee) with the
           exclusive right to sell its product or service in a
           particular territory.
       A franchise is the right to use an established name
           (e.g. Wendy's) or idea to sell particular products
           and/or service.   The chief objective of a fran-
           chise is to facilitate the distribution of the partic-
           ular product or service.

The franchisor advertises its product and provides the franchisee with standard procedures of operation. These may include the franchisor's method of preparing its products, keeping of records and managing employees. In addition, most reputable franchisors provide a training program for its franchisees. Reputable franchisors also provide a proven product or service name, supplies at wholesale and at times various types of financial assistance. This assistance may take the form of a loan, investment capital or a joint venture agreement.

a) Advantages for a small entrepreneur to obtain a franchise:

1. Immediate use of a business organization with an established and hopefully a good reputation.

2. The new owner of a franchise usually receives training in the operation of the business and is then provided help on a continuing basis.

3. The new owner also receives benefits of national advertising and promotional campaigns.

4. Franchisors in many cases, provide financial support for the new owner or can help raise capital because of their reputation.

5. Franchisors provide known products and established methods of doing business which avoid many errors a new owner might make.

b) Costs of obtaining a franchise:

1. Payment of an initial fee - the amount of money paid is dependent upon the nature and reputation of the particular franchise. For example, McDonald's charges a much higher initial fee than many other franchisors because of its known reputation for efficiency and quality.

2. The franchisee may also have to purchase in his fee:
    a. specific equipment
    b. goodwill
    c. other tangible assets the franchisor deems appropriate.
3. Many franchisors require the service to pay a continuous franchise service fee based on a percentage of gross sales or some other particular measure. This is done to pay for such items as advertising, supplies and services.
4. Rules and regulations a franchise must abide by:
    a. Methods of doing business.
    b. Quality of product and/or service.
    c. Design of place of business (e.g. Pizza Hut, McDonald's).
    d. How the business may be sold.

c) Evaluation of a franchise opportunity:
1. Research all information possible about the company.
2. Evaluate all aspects of the business.
3. Get help from a variety of professionals, e.g. accountants, lawyers, analysts, etc.
4. Consult with others who have the franchise and others who are in similar types of business.
5. It is highly recommended that you deal with a franchise that has an established and reputable name.

d) Things to beware of in purchasing a franchise:
1. Fast-talking con artists.
2. Pie-in-the-sky schemes.
3. Shortcuts to fortune.

192

e) Future of franchising:
1. International markets will be opened to franchises.
2. New Marketing methods.
3. New legislation to enhance opportunities in international franchising.
4. New methods of sales promotion.
5. New types of advertising to appeal to the international arena.
f) To achieve the greatest success in a franchise arrangement, it is sometimes imperative for both the franchisor and/or the franchisee to make some compromises. The franchisee surrenders complete control of the business in order to receive the benefits of being part of the franchise operation.
g) Franchising may be a quick way for a small entrepreneur to get into a business but it still requires perseverance, research, determination, and plain old-fashioned hard work.
Some people do not go into franchising because they feel that they do not have the freedom to be as creative as they wish because of the restrictions of the franchisor. However, a franchise does provide the entrepreneur with the opportunity to achieve the profits in conducting the business, any additional profit due to increased value when selling the business, and an opportunity to improve the nature and quality of the business.

X. Sources of Assistance for Small Businesses:
a) SBA - Small Business Administration
b) Small-business investment companies (SBICs)
c) The Sercie Corp of Retired Executives (SCORE)
d) The Active Corps of Exexucitves (ACE)
e) The National Federation of Independent Business
f) The National Small Business Association
g) The Small Business Legislative Council
h) Minority enterprise small-business investment companies (MESBICs)

i) The Inter-racial Council for Business Opportunities (ICBO)
j) The local bank
k) Accountants
l) Lawyers
m) Financial analysts
n) Economists
o) Courses at local colleges
p) Courses provided by the Small Business Administration
q) Pamphlets produced by the Department of Commerce and the Small Business Administration
r) Small Business Institute (SBI) is a program developed by the Small Business Administration
in which advanced business students help
small business by on-site consulting.

XI. The strength of American business is dependent in great
part on the personage of the entrepreneur. Many of
our most successful business enterprises have been
the result of the efforts of the entrepreneur. Most
entrepreneurs will either begin by developing their
own retail, service, manufacturing, wholesale or construction business.

Small businesses can successfully compete in
the marketplace by attracting high-quality people and
emphasizing the opportunity of growing with a smaller company. In addition, the small business is able
to compete because they can respond more quickly to
changes in the marketplace and they can keep their
overhead lower than large companies. Of course,
for a small business to be successful it must be effec-
tively managed and be a product of very careful
planning and organization.

Financing is an important but difficult aspect
of small business. This is due to difficulty of getting loans, paying higher interest than large businesses and having difficulty in attracting venture
capital. Failure to adequately prepare for financing
problems and in general being undercapitalized con-
tributes significantly to small business failures.

In addition, the cause of many small business
failures is poor quality management and inadequate
financing.

However, small business provides the ambitious
entrepreneus with the opportunity of independence,
creativity and a chance to earn a substantial amount

of income. It is an area that many people should seriously consider in their future plans.

QUESTIONS FOR REVIEW AND DISCUSSION

1. What is a small business?

2. Why do people go into small businesses?

3. What type of person is an entrepreneur?

4. How does the Small Business Administration (SBA) assist small business?

5. Describe the basic plan for starting a new business.

6. Discuss the advantages and disadvantages of a small business.

7. Are franchises a good investment? Why?

8. How has the shortage of venture capital caused people to turn to franchising?

9. How does the franchisor usually help a franchisee?

10. How does the franchisor maintain control of the franchisee?

11. Why have the franchises grown in The United States?

12. Why have changes in American customs, working conditions and style of living led to a growth of fast food franchises?

I. Real estate is land and all things attached to that land.
Real estate or real property is immovable property
such as land or buildings.
   a) Real estate is in demand because it is a finite
item. There is a limited amount of land
and because there is a scarcity of land,
there is an increasing demand for the
land.
      1. Desirable land is very much in
demand. Because of this
high demand, prices of desirable land is very high.
      2. Desirable land is a good example
of the law of supply and de-
mand at work.
   b) Land has four major characteristics:
      1. Immovable - land can't be picked up
and taken somewhere else.
      2. Indestructible - land always exists
no matter what has been done to
it.
      3. Heterogeneous - no two pieces of
land are the same. Though they
may look alike, because they are
in different locations they are
different.
      4. Finite - there is a limited amount of
land. One can add to the usa-
bility of land but not to the
amount of land.
   c) Location is the chief factor in evaluating the
dollar value of a home. This is due to:
      1. Quality of life
      2. Neighborhood
      3. Financial status of residents
      4. Zoning laws
      5. Crime statistics
      6. Quality of schools
      7. Transportation
      8. Nearness to places of employment
      9. Recreational features.
   d) The value of land is due to its location and
its potential for development. There are
a number of factors that determine the
location of businesses. They are:

1. Physical resources
2. Human resources
3. Location of market
4. Nearness to energy
5. Quality of transportation
6. Community attitudes
7. Federal governmental policy
8. State governmental policy
9. Local governmental policy
10. Income status of potential customers
11. Incidence of crime.

e) Rental property is different from commercial property.
1. Rental property is made up of apartment buildings, rental homes and condominiums.
2. Commercial property is made up of industrial buildings, malls, shopping centers and office buildings.

II. Mortgage Loans:
a) Mortgage loans are the key ingredient in the financing of homes.
1. Most people obtain a mortgage loan from a bank and use the house as collateral (security) for the loan. If the borrower defaults on the loan, the bank will usually take the property and sell it in order to recover the money.

b) Types of mortgage loans:
1. Fixed mortgage is when the payments remain the same throughout the period of the loan. For example, if interest is 11% per month for thirty years, it will stay at 11% for every monthly payment throughout the period of the loan.
2. Variable mortgage does not have fixed payments throughout the period of the loan. The payments may be changed at various times over the period of the loan. This change may be brought about by changes in the prime interest rate or by another method that the leader and borrower agree upon.

3. <u>Graduated mortgage</u> is a type of mortgage that rises gradually after the first year. After a few years, the rates usually level off.

III. <u>Land Development</u> is an area in which there is an opportunity for acquiring a great deal of income. A land developer will buy underdeveloped land, put homes on it or build industrial buildings on it and then sell it as developed property for a satisfactory profit. One should realize that one does not have to be a large developer in order to earn a substantial income. Some developers are relatively small and develop small parcels of land. However, if the development satisfies the desires of the consumers, the developer, whether large or small, can achieve a great deal of success.

QUESTIONS FOR REVIEW AND DISCUSSION

1. What is real estate?

2. Explain the major characteristics of land.

3. Why is location the primary factor in determining the value of a home?

4. Which are the chief factors in determining the location of a business?

5. How is rental property different from commercial property?

6. Differentiate between fixed, variable and graduated mortgage loans. Which one do you favor?

XXX

RISK MANAGEMENT AND INSURANCE

I. <u>Risk</u> is when one faces the chance of a loss.
    a) There are two types of risks:
       1. <u>Speculative risk</u> is the chance that a company takes in order to achieve a gain. A business person hopes to benefit by taking the risk, but realizes that there is a chance for a loss. A careful businessperson will be able to gauge the amount of loss he will face if his speculative risk does not meet with success.
       2. <u>Pure risk</u> is when there is no possibility of a profit but only the threat of a loss.

II. There are four ways of managing risk:
    a) <u>Risk avoidance</u> is to avoid certain instances that involve the taking of a risk. For example, when one gives up flying in a plan, the risk of dying from a plane crash is avoided.
    b) <u>Risk reduction</u> is the taking of measures which lessens the chance of a certain event occurring. For example, if one gives up smoking, it reduces the risk of lung cancer.
    c) <u>Self-insurance</u> is when a group of companies or a company itself puts money away in order to cover against any possible losses. They set up a special fund into which regular payment is made. This kind of insurance is used in place of coverage by an outside insurance company.
    d) <u>Risk transfer</u> is when the risk is shifted to an insurance firm.

III. An <u>insurance policy</u> is a written contract between an individual or a business firm (known as the "insured") and an insurance company. The insurance company agrees to pay for all or part of a loss in return for a fee.
    a) A <u>premium</u> is the fee paid by a firm or an individual to an insurance company in order to be insured.
    b) <u>Insurable interest</u> is the concept that the insured party (the policyholder) must face a loss, either financial or personal,

because of illness, death, accident, liability, etc. For example, one cannot
take out a policy on someone else's house
because one does not have an insurable
interest in the house.

c) The law of large numbers is a law of probability stating that if a large number of
people or firms are exposed to the same
risk, a predictable number of losses will
occur during a specific period of time.

    1. An actuary figures the degree of
risk involved.

    2. Insurance companies use actuarial
charts to predict the number
of deaths, accidents, fires,
plane crashes, etc., that will
occur in a given period of
time.

    3. The insurance premiums are based
on the law of large numbers.

d) Insurable risks are the risks for which an
insurance policy can be purchased by an
individual or an organization.

    1. In order for the insurance com-
pany to provide protection
against the loss, the loss
must be predictable, acci-
dental, and financially
measurable.

    2. An insurable risk cannot be
caused intentionally by the
insured.

e) Idemnification is an insurance principle which
prevents an insurer from paying to the
insured more than the financial loss that
actually occurred.

    1. One cannot insure a $10,000 auto-
mobile for $75,000 and make a
$65,000 profit if the auto-
mobile was totally demolished.

f) The Law of Adverse Selection states that
people with severe health problems and
those in exceptionally dangerous occu-
pations will probably purchase and renew
health and life insurance policies quicker
than other people.

1. Because of the increased risk the insurance companies will charge these people higher premiums.
2. The insurance companies have the right to determine the standards by which they will issue policies. They also have the right to determine the price of the premium the insured must pay.

g) Redlining is when certain areas are denied a specific type of insurance because the area is considered by the insurance company to be a high risk area. Individual applications for insurance from that area are not considered by the insurance company. The company does not issue certain kinds of policies in that area. For example, some high crime areas of cities cannot get fire and theft insurance coverage from private companies.

IV. Sources of Insurance:
a) Public Insurance companies are government agencies which federal or state governments establish for the purpose of protecting individuals or businesses in a variety of specialized areas that most private insurance companies do not wish to insure.

b) Major types of Public Insurance:
1. Unemployment Insurance provides workers with partial replacement income, and job placement services while they are unemployed.
2. Worker's Compensation Insurance is provided under state law by employers for the purpose of guaranteeing employees protection from the loss of their wages or salary due to injury or illness as a result of employment. This is a state administered program which also provides the employee with rehabilitation services such as retraining and job placement.
3. Social Security is controlled and regulated by the federal government.
   a. Largest insurance program in the United States.

       b. Provides retirement, disability, survivors' and health insurance.

       c. Retirement benefits are paid to the worker based on his or her income during his working years.

       d. If a worker dies before retirement, his survivors will receive the benefits.

       e. Disabled workers collect benefits for periods of long-term disability.

       f. Medicare is a type of health insurance for those over 65 years of age.

c) Other Types of Public Insurance:

    1. Federal Deposit Insurance Corporation (FDIC) and Federal Savings and Loan Insurance Corporation (FSLIC) insures deposits in commercial banks and savings banks.

    2. Mortgage Insurance protects the lender if the borrower defaults on paying the mortgage on his home. This is done by the Federal Housing Administration (FHA).

    3. Flood Insurance is provided by the federal government because private insurance companies refrain from issuing flood insurance policies because floods are natural catastrophes and premiums would not cover costs. The National Flood Insurance Association is the provider in this instance.

    4. Crime Insurance is provided by the federal government if private insurance companies refuse to issue coverage.

    5. Pension Insurance is provided by the federal government and guarantees the payment of pensions if a business goes bankrupt or a pension plan is terminated. The insurer in this case is the Pension Benefit Guaranty Corporation.

    6. Crop Insurance is provided by private insurance companies but the federal government guarantees the coverage.

This is done by the Federal Crop
Insurance Corporation.
d) Private Insurance:
   1. Private Insurance companies may be
       stockholder-owned or mutually owned.
       a. Stock insurance company is
           one whose stock is held
           by the public. One does
           not have to be a policy-
           holder of the insurance
           company to own stock in
           that company. A stock
           insurance company's main
           objective is to achieve a
           profit.
       b. Mutual insurance company is
           one that is owned by its
           policyholders. It does
           not earn profits for its
           owners. Any surplus
           funds are returned to
           the policyholders either
           as dividends or reduc-
           tions in the premiums.
           This type of insurance
           company is found mostly
           in the area of life insur-
           ance.

V. Types of Insurance:
        There are three major types of insurance.
    They are property and liability insurance, health
    insurance and life insurance.
        A. 1. Property insurance covers financial
               losses resulting from physical damage
               to property due to lightning, fire,
               wind, hail, theft, vandalism or other
               forces of destruction.
           2. Liability insurance covers financial losses
               suffered by individuals or business
               organizations should they be held
               responsible for damage to persons or
               property of other people.
           3. Some examples of property and liability
               insurance are fire insurance, auto-
               mobile insurance, theft insurance,
               business interruption insurance, etc.
               a. Fire insurance protects the
                   insured from losses due

203

to fire, water, smoke
damage, etc.
b. Business interruption insurance covers a firm from
losses occurring when a
disaster causes the busi-
ness to close temporarily.
c. Business liability insurance
protects a business
against financial responsibility for another's losses
1. Product liability
insurance
protects the
insured
against claims
for injuries
or damage as
a result of
negligence,
malpractice or
a manufac-
turer's poor
product.
d. Automobile insurance covers
the insured from losses
due to auto theft, fire,
or collision which results
in damage to property or
injury or death to a per-
son.
e. Theft, Burglary and Robbery
insurance covers the
insured for the unlawful
taking of his property.
f. Fidelity bond insures a business from stealing by its
employees.
g. Surety bond is for payment
if a job is not finished
on time. This is often
used in construction
projects.
h. Title insurance insures
against loss due to a
defective title to the land
or other types of proper-
ty such as an automobile.

      i. Credit insurance insures the creditor against the borrower's failure to repay a loan.

      j. Marine insurance insures shippers from losses of property because of damage or theft while a ship is at sea or in port.

      k. Malpractice insurance covers the insured for claims for damages against certain professionals such as physicians.

B. Health insurance is developed to provide insurance coverage for expenses incurred due to sickness or accident. There are a number of kinds of health insurance.

    1. Hospitalization insurance provides coverage for the expenses of being in a hospital. Blue Cross is the largest provider of hospitalization insurance in the United States.

    2. Surgical insurance provides coverage for surgical expenses. Blue Shield is the largest provider of surgical insurance in the United States.

    3. Medical expense insurance is designed to pay for medical expenses other than those dealing with surgery.

    4. Major medical insurance provides insurance against catastrophic financial losses dealing with major illness or injury. This type of insurance usually takes effect when hospitalization insurance and surgical insurance coverage has been exhausted.

    5. Dental and vision insurance covers expenses for dentistry and eye examinations, eyeglasses, contact lenses, etc.

6. <u>Disability income insurance</u> provides income to the insured while he or she is disabled as a result of illness or injury.
7. <u>Health Maintenance Organizations (HMOs)</u> are a prepaid medical plan that provides health services such as clinics and hospitals, to policyholders for a monthly fee.

C. <u>Life Insurance</u> is insurance which upon the death of the insured, pays a set amount of money to the policyholder's beneficiaries. There are three basic forms of life insurance; term life insurance, whole life insurance and endowment life insurance.

1. <u>Term life insurance</u> provides protection for a specific number of years, after which the protection is terminated.
2. <u>Whole life insurance</u> is a combination of insurance protection and the saving of money. This type of insurance policy requires that premiums be paid until the policyholder dies or until he reaches a particular age. The premium payments do not change during the life of the policy.
   a. <u>Straight life insurance</u> pays the face value of the policy to the insured's beneficiary upon the death of the insured.
   b) <u>Universal life insurance</u> is a combination of term insurance with a plan of investment. This type of policy is often used to provide

206

an annuity for
the insured upon
his retirement.
3. <u>Endowment life insurance</u> is more
expensive than whole life
policies. This type of insurance also has a savings com-
ponent. If the insured sur-
vives, he or she receives the
face value of the policy. If
the insured does not survive,
the beneficiaries receive the
face value of the policy.

VI. Business and Life Insurance:
a) Many businesses purchase life insurance for their
employees. They do this by purchasing
<u>group insurance</u> because the rates are less
expensive.
1. Many companies also take out <u>key
person insurance</u> to protect themselves against the loss of essen-
tial employees.
2. Many partnerships and small corporations buy life insurance so their
families can receive the value of
the insured's interest, instead of
the business receiving it.

VII. Why Purchase Insurance?
This portion was contributed by Stuart I. Raphael,
President of Raphael-Scala, Fell & Co., Insur-
ance Adjusters, Hackensack, New Jersey.

We know that insurance is not a tangible item.
You can't see it, smell it, touch it or enjoy playing
with it. Young people just starting out to make
their mark in society are usually under strict budget
constraint and therefore tend to overlook this most
important commodity or purchase only the mandatory
coverages required by the various state regulatory
agencies.
Look at some examples. The most identifiable
would be the young family just starting out where the
sole breadwinner whose wife is a homemaker not gen-
erating an income with two infant children, all being
supported by the single income parent. He is in the
peak of good health, no life insurance was yet purchased. What can happen? He is young and energetic.

Life insurance, though not totally ignored was an item to be put on the backburner until finances were stronger. But one day, while crossing the street, a drunken driver struck him down and he was killed. The wife and children were devastated. There was no more income. The small house had to be sold since the mortgage payments could no longer be met. The wife had to return to work, the children were placed in day care and the family unit was destroyed. Life insurance, if purchased, would have paid off the mortgage, allowed for the hiring of a full time nanny and housekeeper and the payment of continuing bills.

Obvious, yes. An isolated and unique scenario? No.

An apartment dweller without many personal belongings chose not to purchase renters insurance. After all, if there was a fire that destroyed the contents in this apartment or if a burglar stole the stereo equipment, so what. He could eventually replace many of the damaged or stolen items. But the apartment dweller was known to have occasional house parties, inviting his friends often to join him in celebrations. At one such party an event occurred which carried potential lifetime damages. One guest fell on the freshly waxed floor and fractured a hip. Medical expenses totalled in excess of thirty thousand dollars. A lawsuit against the apartment renter was initiated and ultimately the injured party was awarded a quarter of a million dollars from a generous jury. In addition, there were large legal bills. Who pays this? Without insurance, the renter is personally liable and probably pays for the rest of his life with attachment of his salary and this is after all his tangible assets were sold to repay as much as he could immediately. A renter's insurance policy carries liability and medical payment coverage which would have, more than likely, paid for the entire judgement and all legal fees.

The obvious and sometime overlooked insurance coverages which are available to protect a sizeable investment would be those such as an expensive piece (or pieces) of jewelry, a fur coat, a stamp collection, a baseball card collection or a painting. Should these items be damaged, destroyed or stolen, insurance coverages will respond and your cherished items replaced or repaired at no cost other than the premium charge which is normally a minute fraction of the value of the item insured.

A dancer's legs, a pianists hands, a racehorse, a pet, a rain-out of an outdoor affair, trip cancellation and baggage are all items that could be insured.

If something is meaningful to you it should be insured. If there is a possibility of devastating economic exposure to you, insurance should be seriously considered.

Is insurance important? You bet it is.

QUESTIONS FOR REVIEW AND DISCUSSION

1. How can a company manage risk?

2. Explain:

    a) Premium

    b) Law of Large Numbers

    c) Idemnification

    d) Law of Adverse Selection

    e) Redlining

3. How is public insurance different from private insurance?

4. Describe the main types of public insurance.

5. Describe the main types of private insurance.

6. How is Term Life Insurance different from Whole Life Insurance?

7. Why should insurance be purchased?

XXXI

INTERNATIONAL BUSINESS

I. Firms, especially American firms look to get into the
    international trade area because they feel that there
    is a profit to be made in foreign trade.
    a) In dealing with other countries, there is no
        one true way to deal with them. Differ-
        ent countries have different methods of
        doing business and U. S. firms have to
        adopt to their methods.

II. Should a firm go into the international market?
    a) Before going into the international arena a firm
        must decide what its basic mission is.
        1. Is there a need for their goods?
        2. Can they buy goods cheaper in other
            countries?
        3. If they manufacture in a foreign
            country, does it pay for them?
        4. Is the foreign country's political
            situation stable enough to carry
            on business?

III. Key Terms of International Business:
    a) International Business - is any activity of a busi-
        ness that crosses international boundaries.
    b) Multinational corporation - one who operates a
        business in more than one country. e.g. the
        large oil companies.
        1. U. S. multinational corporations are
            very influential in the interna-
            tional business arena.
        2. In general, multinational corporations
            are becoming more and more in-
            ternational in the upper levels of
            management.
    c) Joint Venture - is a type of partnership consist-
        ing of (in an international operation) some
        nationals and some foreigners. In many cases
        it is the U. S. company that puts up the
        capital and citizens of the host country run
        the business. Of course, the American com-
        pany has people there to help operate the
        business.
    d) Branch Office - is an extension of the firm's
        structure. It is an office away from the
        main headquarters of the firm. A branch

office of the firm in the international arena is an office in a foreign country.

e) Dumping - is the practice of selling goods in a foreign country at a lower price than sold domestically. This serves to flood the foreign country with goods.

f) Export Agent - is one who represents several manufacturers in a foreign market.

g) Devaluation - is reducing the value of a nation's currency in relation to the value of another currency.

h) Revaluation - is increasing the value of a nation's currency in relation to the value of another nation's currency.

i) Floating exchange rate - is one that changes depending upon the changing situations of international markets.

j) Subsidiary - is a firm which is owned (over 50%) by another firm. In the arena of international business, the subsidiary is organized under the laws of the nation in which it is conducting its business.

k) International Manager - a manager who is involved in international business activities.

l) Licensing - is the granting by a foreign nation to the firm to produce or distribute its products in that country.

m) Exporting - the selling of a firm's products to other countries.

n) Importing - the purchasing of products from other countries.

o) Balance of Trade - the relation of a nation's exports to imports. If you export more than you import you have a favorable balance of trade and vice-versa.

p) Balance of Payments - all transactions involving imports and exports, investments in plants and equipment, loans made by governments, foreign aid to nations, military spending and money deposits in foreign banks. It measures the amount of money coming into a country against the money going out of the country.

q) Protective Tariffs - a tax on imported goods with the purpose of protecting a nation's products by discouraging imports.

r) Revenue Tariff - a tax on imported goods in order to raise money (revenue).

s) Embargo – is a boycott that does not allow the
        importing of particular products.
t) Theory of Comparative Advantage – is a theory
        stating that each nation should concentrate
        on producing those goods it can supply most
        efficiently and inexpensively compared with
        other nations.
u) Specialization – the practice of a nation producing
        and trading the goods that it can supply most
        inexpensively and efficiently.
v) Capital-Intensive Economy – an economic system
        that uses methods of production that depends
        on large amounts of capital equipment.
w) Labor-Intensive Economy – an economic system
        that uses methods of production that depends
        on a large supply of cheap labor.
x) Tariff – a tax on imports entering the country.
y) International Cartel – a group of sellers of a
        product who join together to control the
        product's price, production and sale in order
        to obtain the advantages of a monopoly.

IV. Three main obstacles that limit the amount of internation-
     al trade.
        a) National Boundaries – distance from other
                countries.
        b) Tariff Barriers – when a nation puts a tax
                (tariff) on imported goods to either raise
                money or protect its own industry or
                both.
        c) Nationalistic Barriers – appeal to national
                pride, loyalty to the workers of the coun-
                try, quotas on imports and embargoes.

V. Free Trade versus Protectionism:
        a) Free Trade advocates believe that those nations
                that can produce particualr items best should
                produce them at the cheapest price and
                should be allowed to sell these items on the
                open market.
        b) Protectionists believe that the country should
                protect its industry and products. They
                want federal laws which serve to protect
                domestic industries from cheaper imported
                goods. Some examples of this are the U. S.
                textile industry and the U. S. auto industry.

VI. Changes in international business over the years:
   a) During the era of European colonization of the
      western hemisphere, international business
      was based on the policy of mercantilism (the
      colonies of the conquering nation exist for
      the benefit of that nation and a nation's
      wealth is measured by the amount of gold and
      silver it possesses).
   b) The nature of international business was to ex-
      ploit the colonies for the benefit of the mother
      country.
         a. Colonies as a source for raw materials.
         b. Colonies as a source of cheap labor.
         c. Colonies as a market for the nation's
            finished products.
   c) Individuals who served in the colonies carried
      the nation's culture to the outposts. This
      was very evident in the case of England and
      France in their colonies in Asia, North and
      South America and Africa.
   d) The nationals serving in the colonies, along with
      the military saw as their purpose the protec-
      tion of their nation's interests. However,
      the natives in the colonies began resenting
      the domination by the powerful nation and
      wanted an end to being exploited.
         1. Therefore, a gradual accommodation
            was made. Some mutual cooper-
            ation between the powerful nation
            and the colony was developed.
         2. Because (even after gaining indepen-
            dence) the colony or former
            colony needed the powerful coun-
            try's money, technological know-
            how and economic understanding;
            some sort of compromise was
            agreed to with each country be-
            coming a partner in the various
            business enterprises.
         3. Eventually, the strong companies of
            the powerful country were re-
            placed by multinational corpora-
            tions in which the powerful
            country's executives are used in
            top management positions while
            the local people are used in low-
            er positions.

213

VII.   Advantages and Disadvantages of International Business:

<table>
<tr><td><u>Advantages</u></td><td><u>Disadvantages</u></td></tr>
</table>

Advantages	Disadvantages
(1) High rate of profit.	(1) Low rate of profit.
(2) Stability.	(2) Forced into a joint venture that is high risk.
(3) Learning a foreign culture.	
(4) Cooperation with foreign governments.	(3) Methods of doing business in the other country that is harmful to the firm.
(5) New areas of developments.	(4) Possibility of nationalizing the business.
	(5) Need to adopt to foreign culture.
	(6) Red-tape.
	(7) Interference of foreign government.

VIII.   Type of people assigned to international positions:
      a) Should be experienced.
      b) Should be mature.
      c) Should be tolerant.
      d) Should be willing to learn about other cultures.
      e) Should enjoy traveling.
      f) Should have a great degree of competency in their particular field.
      g) Should be optimistic.
      h) Should be able to have others trust him or her.

IX.   Conflicts of cultures affects international managers.
      a) When managers deal in a different culture, they face different methods of doing things and different expectations. They must adapt to these differences and make the necessary adjustments in order to successfully conduct the business of the firm.
      b) Cultural Differences
          1. <u>Ethnocentrism</u> - is the using of one's own culture as the criteria of reference in dealing with a foreign culture.
              a. If this is done by international managers it will most likely be resented

by the native population
and harm business.

    b. A different value system has
to be adjusted to the
foreign value system. If
this can be done, the
firm stands a chance for
greater success. If it
can't, then the chance
for success is greatly
diminished.

2. Religious differences - different religious
customs can have a great effect on
the firm's business.

3. Differences in customs and various society's norms of behavior contribute
to cultural differences.

4. The international manager's inability to
adjust to, or unwillingness to adjust
to cultural differences often cause
difficulties.

    a. harms relations with local
personnel of firm.

    b. harms relations with local
customers of firm.

    c. harms relations with local
government of host
country.

X. Economic Differences:

    a) Technological differences - different nations are
in different situations in regard to the degree of development in the technological area.

    b) Economic philosophy - differences in economic
philosophy can influence the host nation's
treatment of the firm.

    c) Demographic influences - differences in the influ-
ence of population can also influence the host
nation's treatment of the company.

    d) Standard of living of the native population - if a
host nation has a much lower standard of
living it can lead to a great deal of resent-
ment towards the firm of the investor nation.

    e) Modes of labor of the native work force - if the
host nation has people who are only able to
do menial labor and cannot handle some of
the modern equipment, the investor company
has to invest a great deal of time, effort and

money in order to train a productive labor force.

 f) <u>Rate of productivity of work force</u> - if the host nation has a work force that is highly productive, it will encourage foreign investment to build industry there and vice-versa.

 g) <u>Rate of currency exchange</u> - if the investor nation gets a good rate of exchange in the host country, it will be a source of encouragement to do business in that country.

XI. Political Differences:

 a) The nature of the international political scene can have a great effect on the success of a firm. For example, when Fidel Castro came to power in Cuba, he nationalized a number of businesses owned by U. S. firms.

 b) <u>Foreign policy</u> - the foreign policy of the U. S. can effect the firm. For instance, the government might not want a firm to do business in a particular country or may not want them to send certain types of products to that country. The U. S. government does not want U. S. firms to export high technological items to The Soviet Union.

 c) <u>National prejudices</u> - this can vary as the international scene will vary.

XII. Currency Valuation:

 a) <u>Exchange rate</u> - is the value of one nation's currency as measured against another nation's currency - e.g. one U. S. dollar will purchase four German marks.

  1. A <u>strong</u> U. S. dollar will buy a large amount of a particular foreign currency.

  2. A <u>weak</u> U. S. dollar will buy a smaller amount of a particular foreign currency.

 b) The strength of the U. S. dollar has an affect on the amount of U. S. exports and imports.

  1. If the value of the dollar is <u>lower</u>, the U. S. will have more exports because foreign countries can more easily afford to purchase U. S. goods.

  2. If the value of the dollar is <u>higher</u>, the U. S. will have more imports

because we can more easily afford
to purchase foreign goods.
- c) Imbalance occurs when one nation's currency increases or decreases too much in value when
compared to the currency of another nation.
Since the mid-1980's, the U. S. dollar has
lost a great deal of value as compared to the
Japanese yen.
  1. The free market solution for correct-
  ing an imbalance in payments, is
  to increase exports to the nation
  which has the favorable balance
  of payments (more exports than
  imports - therefore, more money
  is going into the country, than is
  going out of the country). Because of this, the U. S. should
  sell Japan more of the products
  in which it has a comparative advantage so that the U. S. may
  be able to reduce its trade deficit with Japan.
  2. The United States may be able to
  alter its unfavorable (deficit)
  balance of payments by:
    a. Reducing its overseas
       military expenditures
    b. Reducing foreign aid
    c. Reducing foreign travel
    d. Reducing its overseas
       investments.

XIII. Tariffs and Trade Barriers:
Though there is a strong movement throughout the
world toward free trade, it appears that it will be a very
long time, if ever, before world wide free trade occurs.
In the meantime there are a number of trade barriers in
existence which attempt to give a trade advantage to the
industries of the home country.
- a) Tariffs are taxes that are levied on imported
products for the purpose of raising money
and protecting domestic (local) industry from
competition from foreign countries.
  1. Revenue tariffs - see this chapter
  part III #r.
  2. Protective tariffs - see this chapter
  part III #q.

b) <u>Import quotas</u> place a limit on the amount of specific kinds of goods that are allowed to be brought into the country. The purpose of import quotas is to protect domestic industry from foreign competition.

c) An <u>embargo</u> as stated earlier, is a boycott on the importing and exporting of specific goods. For example, the United States, before the War of 1812, placed an embargo on trade with Great Britain and France.

d) <u>Exchange control</u> is when a government attempts to regulate foreign exchange. This is done in order to help carry out the formulations of its foreign and domestic policy. This is done through a nation's national or central bank. All companies must sell or purchase foreign currency through the national or central bank. This enables the nation to regulate foreign exchange according to their national desires.

XIV. Trade Agreements

A <u>trade agreement</u> is a commercial treaty entered into by nations for the purpose of regulating trade between the nations. Trade agreements are entered into for a variety of reasons, but mainly for economic and/or political motives. The United States has entered into many commercial treaties with other nations. For example, the U. S. gives some nations <u>favored nation status</u>, thereby giving these nations special trade privileges.

a) <u>Common Market</u> (European Economic Community - EEC) was formed in 1958 by the Treaty of Rome. By this treaty, the countries of Western Europe agreed to permit free trade among the member nations. This free trade agreement is credited, in large part, for the economic growth and development of Western Europe.

b) <u>General Agreements on Tariffs and Trade (GATT)</u> were first developed in 1959 and are international trade agreements that attempt to lower tariff and trade restrictions throughout the world. There are periodic GATT negotiations with more and more nations entering into the agreements. Presently, there are nearly 100 nations that have signed the GATT accords.

c) <u>Free trade areas</u> are entered into by various
groups of nations. This allows the members
of the group to trade amongst themselves
free from any tariffs or trade barriers.

V. Multinational Corporations

As stated before, a multinational corporation is one
who operates a business in more than one country. However, multinational corporations are more than that. The
multinational corporations look at the world as their
marketplace. Some people state that a multinational corporation must have operations in a minimum of six countries, have sales over $100 million and have its subsidi-
aries which are located in foreign countries, account for
a substantial portion of their assets.

Multinational corporations are presently undergoing
close scrutiny because many people see them as existing
outside of national interests. For example, many Americans claim that the large oil companies show more loyalty
and consideration to their international interests than to
policies that benefit the people of the United States.
This feeling was brought about, in part, by the oil short-
ages of 1973, 1979 and the Exxon oil spill in Alaska in
1989.

However, there are disagreements over the advantages and disadvantages of multinational corporations.

Advantages	Disadvantages
a) Encourages economic growth.	a) Multinationals are too powerful.
b) Encourages peaceful relations.	b) Disrupt national economies.
c) Improves technology and development on an international scale.	c) Multinationals have more loyalty to themselves than their nation.
d) Capital, information and goods are transferred to many nations.	d) The transference of capital, information and goods to other nations damages the national economy
	e) Multinationals believe they are above the law of nations
	f) Multinationals have too much influence.

219

QUESTIONS FOR REVIEW AND DISCUSSION

1. Why does a firm go into international business?

2. Explain:
   - a) joint venture
   - b) multinational corporation
   - c) balance of trade
   - d) economic boycott
   - e) balance of payments
   - f) free trade
   - g) protectionism
   - h) dumping
   - i) devaluation
   - j) theory of comparative advantage
   - k) labor-intensive economy

3. How can international business benefit a firm?

4. Which type of people are best suited to positions in international business?

5. How do cultural differences influence the international manager's actions?

6. How do economic differences influence the actions of the international manager?

7. How do political differences affect the actions of the international manager?

8. How can the strength of the U. S. dollar affect the amount of U. S. exports and imports?

9. How can a nation change its unfavorable balance of payments?

10. Why are trade agreements important to a nation's economic health?

11. Why have multinational corporations been the subject of criticism?

12. Are multinational corporations a benefit or a harm to the United States?

13. How should the United States deal with multinational corporations? Should they be more strictly regulated? Should there be less regulation? Explain your position.

SELECTED BIBLIOGRAPHY

BOOKS

Amling, Frederick. Investments. 6th Edition. Englewood
Cliffs, N. J.: Prentice-Hall, 1988.

Antony, Jay. Management and Machiavelli. New York: Holt,
Rinehart and winston, 1967.

Argyris, Chris. Personality and Organization: The Conflict
Between the System and the Individual. New York: Harper
& Row, 1057.

Barnard, C. I. The Functions of the Executive. Cambridge,
Mass.: Harvard University Press, 1938.

Baty, Gordon B. Entrepreneurship for the Eighties. Reston,
Va.: Reston Publishing Co., Inc., 1981.

Bautier, Robert-Henri. The Economic Development of Medieval
Europe. London: Harcourt, Brace, Jovanovich, Inc., 1971.

Beaton, William R. Real Estate Finance. Englewood Cliffs,
N. J.: Prentice-Hall, Inc., 1975.

Bedeian, Arthur G. and Glueck, William F. Management.
Hinsdale, Ill.: Dryden Press, 1983.

Blake, Robert R. and Mouton, Jane S. The Managerial Grid.
Houston: Gulf Publishing Co.: 1964.

Boone, Louis E. and Kurtz, David L. Contemporary Marketing.
Hinsdale, Illinois: The Dryden Press, 1974.

Boone, Louis E. and Kurtz, David L. Principles of Management,
2nd Edition. New York: Random House, 1984.

Carroll, Jr., Stephen J. and Tosi, Jr., Henry L. Management
by Objectives: Applications and Research. New York:
Macmillan & Co., 1973.

Chamberlain, John. The Roots of Capitalism. Princeton, N. J.:
D. Van Nostrand Co., Inc., 1965.

Chase, Richard B. and Aquilano, Nicholas. Production/Operations Management, 4th Edition. Homewood, Illinois: Richard D. Irwin, 1985.

Cleland, David I. and King, William R. Systems Analysis and Project Management. New York: McGraw-Hill Book Co., 1968.

Cohen, Jerome B., Zinbarg, Edward D. and Zeikel, Arthur. Investment Analysis and Portfolio Management, 3rd Edition. Homewood, Illinois: Richard D. Irwin, Inc., 1977.

Cohen, Sanford. Labor in the United States. Columbus, Ohio: Charles E. Merrill Books, Inc., 1960.

Coman, Katherine B. The Industrial History of the United States. New York: The Macmillan Company, 1917.

Compaine, Benjamin M. and Litro, Robert F. Business: An Introduction. New York: The Dryden Press, 1984.

Cox, Keith K. and Enis, Ben M. The Marketing Research Process. Pacific Palisades, Calif.: Goodyear Publishing Co., 1972.

Dale, Ernest. Management: Theory and Practice. New York: McGraw-Hill Book Co., 1965.

Davis, R. C. The Fundamentals of Top Management. New York: Harper & Brothers, 1951.

DeBono, Peter and Laurie, Peter. The Beginner's Guide to Computers. Reading, Mass.: Addison-Wesley, 1982.

Drucker, Peter F. The Practice of Management. New York: Harper & Row, 1954.

Drucker, Peter F. Concept of the Corporation. New York: The John Day Company, 1972.

Eichler, Ned. The Merchant Builders. Cambridge, Massachusetts: The M.I.T. Press, 1982.

Faulkner, Harold Underwood. American Economic History, 8th Edition. New York: Harper & Brothers, 1960.

Fayol, Henri. General and Industrial Management. London: Pitman Publishing Corp., 1949.

222

Fess, Philip E. and Niswonger, C. Rollin. Accounting Principles, 13th Edition. Cincinnati, Ohio: South-Western Publishing Co., 1981.

Fiedler, Fred E. A Theory of Leadership Effectiveness. New York: McGraw-Hill Book Co., 1967.

Flamholtz, Eric. How to Make the Transition from an Entrepreneurship to a Professionally Managed Firm. San Francisco: Jossey-Bass, 1987.

Friedman, Milton. Capitalism and Freedom. Chicago: University of Chicago Press, 1962.

Friedman, Milton & Rose. Free to Choose. New York: Avon Books, 1981.

Gantt, Henry L. Organizing for Work. London: George Allen and Unwin, 1919.

Geneen, Harold. Managing. New York: Doubleday & Co., 1984.

Gilder, George. Wealth and Poverty. New York: Basic Books, 1981.

Gillespie, Karen R. and Hecht, Joseph C. Retail Business Management, 2nd Edition. New York: McGraw-Hill Book Company, 1977.

Griffin, Rickey E. and Ebert, Ronald J. Business. Englewood Cliffs, N. J.: Prentice-Hall, 1989.

Halloran, John A., Lanser, Howard P. Introduction to Financial Management. Glenview, Illinois: Scott, Foresman & Co., 1985.

Hampton, John J. Financial Decision-Making. Reston, Va.: Reston Publishing Co., 1976.

Hays, Samuel P. The Response to Industrialism. Chicago: The University of Chicago Press, 1957.

Heilbroner, Robert L. The Worldly Philosophers, 3rd Edition, New York: Simon and Schuster, 1968.

Heimann, Eduard. History of Economic Doctrines. New York: Oxford University Press, 1964.

223

Herzberg, Frederick, Mausner, B. and Snyderman, B. The Motivation to Work. New York: John Wiley and Sons, 1959.

Ivancevich, John M., Lyon, Herbert L. and Adams, David P. Business In A Dynamic Environment. New York: West Publishing Co., 1979.

Keynes, John Maynard. The General Theory. New York: Harcourt, Brace & World, Inc., 1964.

Kotler, Philip. Marketing Management, 6th Edition. Englewood Cliffs, N. J.: Prentice-Hall, 1988.

Kohn, Mervin. Dynamic Managing. Menlo Park, California: Cummings Publishing Co., Inc., 1977.

Krooss, Herman E. and Gilbert, Charles. American Business History. Englewood Cliffs, N. J.: Prentice-Hall, Inc., 1972.

Likert, Rensis. New Patterns of Management. New York: McGraw-Hill Book Co., 1961.

Litwin, George H. and Stringer, Jr., Robert A. Motivation and Organizational Climate. Boston: Division of Research, Graduate School of Business Administration, Harvard University, 1968.

Longenecker, Justin G. Essentials of Management. Columbus, Ohio: Charles E. Merrill Publishing Co., 1977.

Maier, Norman R. Psychology in Indistrial Organizations. Boston, Mass.: Houghton-Mifflin & Co., 1973.

Marx, Karl. Das Kapital. Chicago: Henry Regnery Company, 1959.

Maslow, Abraham H. Motivation and Personality. New York: Harper and Brothers, 1954.

Mayo, Elton. The Human Problems of an Industrial Civilization. Boston: Division of Research, Harvard Business School, 1945.

Mayo, Herbert B. Finance: An Introduction, 2nd Edition. New York: The Dryden Press, 1982.

McClelland, David C. The Achieving Society. Princeton, N. J.:
Van Nostrand, 1961.

McGregor, Douglas. The Human Side of Enterprise. New York:
McGraw-Hill Book Co., 1960.

McGregor, Douglas. The Professional Manager. New York:
McGraw-Hill Book Co., 1967.

Murphy, Edward F. Management vs. The Unions. New York:
Stein and Day, 1971.

Needles, Jr., Belverd E., Anderson, Henry R. and Caldwell,
James C. Principles of Accounting, 3rd Edition. Boston:
Houghton-Mifflin Co., 1987.

Newman, William H. and Warren, E. Kirby. The Process of
Management, 4th Edition. Englewood Cliffs, N. J.:
Prentice-Hall, 1977.

Ouchi, William G. Theory Z. Reading, Mass.: Addison-Wesley,
1981.

Peters, Thomas J. and Waterman, Jr., Robert H. In Search of
Excellence. New York: Harper & Row, 1982.

Rachman, David J. and Mescon, Michael H. Business Today,
4th Edition. New York: Random House, Inc., 1985.

Rayback, Joseph G. A History of American Labor. New York:
The Free Press, 1966.

Reynolds, Lloyd G. Labor Economics and Labor Relations.
Englewood Cliffs, N. J.: Prentice-Hall, Inc., 1978.

Ritter, Lawrence S. and Silber, William L. Money, Banking
and Financial Markets, 6th Edition. New York: Basic
Books, Inc., 1989.

Rostow, W. W. The Stages of Economic Growth. New York:
Oxford Unviersity Press, 1965.

Samuelson, Paul A. and Nordhaus, William D. Economics, 12th
Edition. New York: McGraw-Hill Book Co., 1985.

Schumpater, Joseph A. The Theory of Economic Development.
New York: Oxford University Press, 1961.

Schuler, Randall S., Beutell, Nicholas J. and Youngblood,
Stuart A. Effective Personnel Management, 3rd Edition.
New York: McGraw-Hill Book Co., 1985.

Skinner, B. F. Science and Human Behavior. New York: The
Free Press, 1953.

Smith, Adam. Wealth of Nations. New York: Modern Library,
1937.

Stanton, William J. and Buskirk, Richard H. Management of the
Sales Force. Homewood, Ill.: Richard D. Irwin, Inc., 1974.

Stanton, William J. and Futrell, Charles. Fundamentals of
Marketing, 8th Edition. New York: McGraw-Hill Book Co.,
1987.

Surry, Stanley S., Warren, William C., McDaniel, Paul R. and
Ault, Hugh J. Federal Income Taxation, Vol. I. Mineola,
New York: The Foundation Press, Inc., 1972.

Taylor, Frederick W. The Principles of Scientific Management.
New York: Harper and Brothers, 1911.

Tschan, Francis J., Grimm, Harold J. and Squires, J. Duane.
Western Civilization Since 1500. New York: J. B. Lippincott Co., 1947.

U. S. Constitution, 1787.

U. S. Department of Commerce. Franchise Opportunities Hand-
book, 1983.

U. S. Government Printing Office. Statistical Abstract of the
United States. Published yearly.

von Bertalanffy, Ludwig. General Systems Theory. New York:
George Braziller, 1969.

Vroom, Victor H. Work and Motivation. New York: J. Wiley
and Sons, Inc., 1964.

Vroom, Victor H. and Yetton, Philip W. Leadership and Decision-Making. Pittsburgh: University of Pittsburgh Press,
1973.

Weber, Max. The Protestant Ethic and the Spirit of Capitalism.
New York: Charlest Scribner's Sons, 1958.

Wechman, Robert J. Encountering Management. Champaign,
   Illinois: Stipes Publishing Co., 1988.

Woodward, Joan. Industrial Organization: Theory and Practice.
   London: Oxford University Press, 1965.

Wren, Daniel A. The Evolution of Management Thought. New
   York: Ronald Press, 1972.

ARTICLES

Blake, Robert R., Mouton, Jane S., Barnes, Louis B. and
   Grenier, Larry E. "Breakthrough in Organization Development." Harvard Business Review (Nov.-Dec., 1964), 133-
   155.

Carlucci, Frank C. "Global Economic Order-Facing the Chal-
   lenge," Sloan Management Review (Spring, 1985), 65-68.

Clouser, Christopher E. "Corporate Support of Education:
   Some Ideas for Advancing Science Literacy," New Jersey Bell
   Journal (Winter-Spring, 1988-1989), 26-35.

Doyle, Stephen X. and Shapiro, Benson P. "What Counts Most
   in Motivating Your Sales Force?" Harvard Business Review
   (May-June, 1980), 133-140.

Drucker, Peter F. "The Re-industrialization of America," Wall
   Street Journal (June 13, 1980), 10.

Gellerman, Saul W. "Why 'Good' Managers Make Bad Ethical
   Choices." Harvard Business Review (July-August, 1986),
   85-90.

Greenwood, Ronald C. "Management by Objectives: As Developed by Peter Drucker, assisted by Harold Smiddy."
   Academy of Management Review (April, 1981), 225-230.

Grenier, Larry E. "Patterns of Organization Change." Harvard Business Rewiv (May-June, 1967), 119-130.

Henry, Porter. "Manage Your Sales Force as a System." Harvard Business Review (March-April, 1975), 89-95.

Koontz, Harold. "The Management Theory Jungle." Journal of
   the Academy of Management (Vol. 4, No. 3), 174-188.

Kotkin, Joel and Kishimoto, Yoriko, "Theory F", Inc. (April, 1986), 52-60.

Levinson, Harry. "Management by Whose Objectives." Psychological Review (July, 1943), 370-396.

McKenney, James L. and Keen, Peter G. W. "How Manager's Minds Work." Harvard Business Review (April, 1981), 225-230.

Podhoretz, Norman. "The New Defenders of Capitalism." Harvard Business Review (March-April, 1981), 96-106.

Richardson, Peter R. and Gordon, John R. M. "Measuring Total Manufacturing Performance," Sloan Management Review (Winter, 1980), 47-58.

Ross, Irwin. "How Lawless Are Big Companies?" Fortune (December 1, 1980), 57-64.

Schein, Edgar H. "Management as a Process of Influence." Industrial Management Review (May, 1961), 59-76.

Suczewski, Janice. "Plan to Succeed." Executive Business Magazine (January-February, 1988), 31-34.

Tannenbaum, Robert and Schmidt, Warren H. "How to Choose a Leadership Pattern." Harvard Business Review (March-April, 1958), 95-101.

Vernon, Raymond. "Can U. S. Manufacturing Come Back?" Harbard Business Review (July-August, 1986), 98-106.

Welch, Joe L. and Gordon, David. "Assessing the Impact of Flexitime on Productivity." Business Horizons (December, 1980), 61-65.

Wilson, Erika. "Social Responsibility of Business: What Are the Small Business Perspectives?" Journal of Small Business Management (July, 1980), 17-24.

PERIODICALS

The Wall Street Journal

Forbes

Barron's

Boardroom Reports

Business Week

Inc.

Fortune

Journal of Accountancy

Harvard Business Review

Journal of Business

Journal of Marketing

Nation's Business

Survey of Current Business

Financial Executive

Financial Management

Journal of Small Business
  Management

Executive Business Magazine

Business Horizons

Dun's Business Monthly

Sloan Management Review

Nation's Business

Entrepreneurship